Making Mergers Work
A Guide to Managing Mergers and Acquisitions

D0959491

International rights and foreign translations available only through
negotiation with Pritchett, LLC.

ISBN 0-944002-21-8

Library of Congress Catalog Card No. 86-73001

Printed in the United States of America

P R I T C H E T T

Making Mergers Work
A Guide to Managing Mergers and Acquisitions

Price Pritchett

To Mother and Dad

A merger is a process, not an event.

The integration period for an acquisition will be measured by months and perhaps years, rather than days or weeks. Many factors come into play in determining what the time frame will be:

1. Whether the merger/acquisition event is a Rescue, Collaboration, Contested Situation, or Raid.
2. The extent to which the two organizations will be merged and integrated.
3. Managerial competency and experience base of the people in charge.
4. Cultural differences of the two organizations.
5. External events in the economy or business world at large.
6. The degree to which the integration program proceeds in a strategic, informed manner.

Companies need to be as willing to spend money on fighting to make a merger work as they are on (a) fighting to keep it from happening or (b) fighting to make it happen. It's time for post-merger management to become as sophisticated as today's take-over plans and merger defenses.

Invariably, companies spend a great deal of money in swinging the deal. For example, there are investment bankers to pay, lawyers' fees, expenses incurred in public relations activities, and so on. But after the papers have been signed, companies frequently quit spending money on expert help, relying instead on incumbent managers and executives who have not been trained for the complicated task of merger integration.

Often, more money is spent changing the company stationery and putting up a new sign out front than is invested in bringing state-of-the-art management techniques to the merger.

A large corporation wouldn't think of spending $50 million or $200 million, maybe even a billion dollars, buying new machinery and putting it in the hands of people who'd never operated that kind of equipment. Obviously, too much would be at stake. Specialized and in-depth training would be given to the persons responsible for making the machines produce.

But every day companies spend that much money and more on an acquisition—sometimes in an unrelated field—and then dump it on executives who have never run that type of operation or that large an organization.

On-the-job training is great, but not for mergers. It gets very expensive when managers take a trial-and-error approach in their efforts to integrate an acquisition.

Managers and executives will be well-intentioned and will give it their best shot, but it takes more than the "old college try." It takes insight into the complicated dynamics of mergers.

Mergers call for many "counterintuitive" moves, such that the people in charge must be very leery of trusting their instincts. Too often the people in charge take the obvious, common sense steps . . . that just happen to be dead wrong.

Since mergers represent unconventional growth, they call for unconventional solutions.

Mergers are very destabilizing events, and they create a phenomenal opportunity for change and performance improvement in organizations. But the upheaval must be managed astutely.

Employees need to understand what the predictable merger dynamics are so they can flow with them. Managers at all levels need to know what's happening, what top executives have as a game plan, so they can manage the situation. Finally, everyone needs to know how they personally will be affected so they can begin to adjust as quickly as possible.

This implies that all the acquired employees, possibly those in the parent company as well, need to be informed about merger dynamics. They need to be trained and coached on what's coming at them.

The managers must be kept informed. Nobody does a good job of managing when they have to do it in the dark.

Finally, since people need personal closure on job-oriented issues, personnel decisions should be made and communicated as rapidly as possible.

At the risk of oversimplifying things, there are three basic laws for successful mergers:

1. *Give the people good reasons for wanting it to work.* If the people who still have jobs want the merger to work, there's a good chance it will. If they don't want it to work or don't care, the odds change dramatically. The issue here is motivation.

2. *Show the people how to make it work.* Employees at all levels need training and coaching, from top executives struggling to manage transition and change, to the rank-and-file employees confused by cultural differences and new procedures. They will be asking, "What do I need to do? How do I handle this?"

3. *Check to see if it is working.* Mergers need to be monitored. There is always some fine-tuning that is needed, some calibrating and correcting of problems. Expect it. There will be breakdowns. Problems will develop. That's acceptable. What's not acceptable is not knowing there are problems or not taking care of them.

When these laws are violated, it tears organizations apart. They get "mergerized"—run through the corporate blender where the value of the deal gets chewed to bits.

It seems impossible that everyone involved can remain completely satisfied when firms are being acquired and merged. But neither does it seem that job stress should measure a 10 on the Richter scale. Surely mergers can be achieved without bankrupting morale, destroying so many careers, or causing so much damage to corporate momentum.

Some of the answer lies in knowing, and respecting, the outrageous costs associated with mergers that are poorly managed. Another part of the answer lies in knowing the problems that must be faced, and the most common management traps. Finally, the last part of the answer lies in knowing the things that do work, and the timing for making them work.

This book is aimed at providing the answer.

ACKNOWLEDGMENTS

I would like to express deep appreciation to Joyce Ferguson, manager of our support staff at Pritchett and Associates, Inc., for spearheading the book's production effort. She hammered out the manuscript in record time, offering unqualified support along with invaluable critique and suggestions for improvements. Diana Nestler also played a special role in fine-tuning the book's grammar and composition. Gayla Weatherford and Linda Roberge are due thanks for pitching in during the final stages of proofing and production. Dr. Ron Pound, Fred Cover, and Debra Williams carried the ball on our consulting projects so I would have the necessary writing time. Altogether they make a remarkable team.

Finally, I've got to say thanks to Patty and the kids—Julie, Price, and Kim. Wherever I wanted to hole up at the house and dictate, they respected my privacy. They, too, are an outstanding team.

Price Pritchett

MERGERIZED!

The announcement flatly stated,
"No change is anticipated."
And the *Journal*, on perusal,
Promised, "Business as usual."

Some saw that as wishful thinking,
Others soaked it up, unblinking—
But no one fully realized
That soon they would be MERGERIZED!

Then employees grew uncertain;
Ambiguity, like a curtain,
Hid the future, made things vague—
Fear gripped some folks like the plague.

Work was really not much fun—
No one trusted anyone.
That was when they first surmised
They were being MERGERIZED!

Top brass stonewalled it at first,
Then said, "Look, we're past the worst."
But talk is cheap, and doesn't sell
When things are going straight to hell.

The casualties began to mount,
And people watched the body count.
With apprehension in their eyes
They talked of being MERGERIZED!

Some bailed out and some were fired,
Others took cash and retired.
Those who stayed were down and out,
Mad as fire, or in a pout.

Low morale and high confusion
Led to problems in profusion.
Now it couldn't be disguised—
They had just been MERGERIZED!

This routine went on for ages,
Through the grief and mourning stages—
Good careers went up in smoke,
And shareholders were going broke.

When faith and hope had run their course,
The marriage ended in divorce.
No one should really be surprised . . .
That's life, when firms get MERGERIZED!

—Price Pritchett

CONTENTS

CHAPTER ONE

Cutting the High Cost of Mismanaged Mergers

Growth through mergers and acquisitions is a high-stakes game.

The element of risk adds to the drama, excitement, and overall appeal of the game. But as always, where there is much to be gained, there is a precipitous downside risk as well.

The gamble becomes a safer one to the extent that companies prepare themselves properly for corporate marriage. This involves a number of preparatory steps:

1. Developing organizational self-insight, such that managers and executives understand their own compatibility as a merger partner.
2. Determining what the new financial demands or considerations will be, and how they can be successfully handled.
3. Thinking strategically about the kind of partner it will require for the relationship to survive over time.
4. Purposefully and proactively looking for such a potential partner, and creating options to choose from.
5. Investing the necessary time in organizational courtship prior to the merger ceremony.

The huge sums of money invested in a merger/acquisition partner are most at risk, though, after the deal is done. In fact, the closing is just the beginning.

THE FAILURE RATE IN TODAY'S MERGER WORLD

A generous number of studies have been conducted by credible researchers on the success and failure rates of merger/acquisition events. The results vary somewhat, but none are encouraging enough to excite the highly conservative investor.

Overall, the critique shows that companies may have as much as a fifty-fifty chance of achieving a successful merger, with the worst case findings showing up to 80 percent of all mergers being disappointments.

Many companies, however, keep turning a deaf ear toward these statistics. This is shown by the continuing growth in the number of merger/acquisition deals each year and the size of the deals that are being struck.

Either somebody doesn't believe the numbers, or the world still contains a lot of gambling men.

Undoubtedly some company owners and executives don't really take the time to calculate the odds. They want to grow; when what looks like a good opportunity comes along, they seize it. Sometimes it works, sometimes it doesn't. That's business.

Other corporate bosses know what the numbers say. But they exhibit an adult version of the "invulnerable adolescent syndrome." Presuming themselves to be bulletproof, they fully believe themselves good enough at what they do to beat the published odds. And some of them are that good. Some are great.

But it should be a sobering fact to note that the statistics on merger success aren't really showing any discernible improvement. With all the innovative takeover plans and the growing sophistication in merger defenses, there simply has not been a corresponding improvement in merger integration efforts.

A cover story in *Business Week* raised the question, "Do Mergers Really Work?" The conclusion:

> In an era of ever-increasing and ever-bigger mergers, a remarkable number—somewhere between a half and two thirds—simply don't work . . . one out of three acquisitions is later undone . . . The selloffs, spinoffs, and writeoffs don't tell the whole story of corporate takeovers gone awry. Many are dying a slow death.[1]

---

[1]Steven Prokesch and Teresa Carson, "Do Mergers Really Work?" *Business Week*, June 3, 1985, pp. 88-89.

Merger failure is not just the curse of the smaller companies with less professional management and more meager financial resources. The rich and famous fail too.

Again and again the corporate giants have made their contributions to the merger/acquisition failure statistics. Their vulnerability has been demonstrated in unsuccessful acquisitions both large and small:

> Coca-Cola, acquiring Wine Spectrum
> Baldwin-United, acquiring MGIC Investment
> Westinghouse Electric, acquiring Teleprompter
> Atlantic Richfield, acquiring Anaconda Minerals
> Philip Morris, acquiring Seven-Up
> Mobil, acquiring Montgomery Ward (Marcor) and Container
>   Corporation of America
> General Electric, acquiring Utah International
> Schlumberger, acquiring Fairchild

Even proud and mighty Exxon was humbled in the rather large Reliance Electric acquisition as well as its purchase of little Vydec.

Richard B. Mann, writing in the *Merger Management Report*, offers an interesting comparison:

> New businesses, many started by people who have never been in business before, are, on average, more successful than mergers by seasoned professionals.[2]

Mann writes that approximately 700,000 new businesses were started during 1985, with some 10 percent of these failing. The failure rate was one out of three for venture capital start-ups.

By contrast, Mann points out that there were 1,237 divestitures in the total 3,001 merger transactions reported in 1985 by the Chicago firm of W. T. Grimm. These divestitures represent 4 percent of the total transactions during 1985. Mann states that the average failure rate for each of the previous five years was about 36 percent of all transactions. But he states,

> When divestitures are compared with acquisitions for 1985, the rate is 70 percent.[3]

---

[2]Richard B. Mann, *Merger Management Report* (Ipswich, Mass.: Cambridge Corporation, July, 1986), p. 1.
[3]Ibid.

But the purpose of this book is not to argue against growth through mergers and acquisitions. Some of those deals pan out beautifully. And many others that fail, or that struggle along with only mediocre results, could also be gloriously successful if the quality of postmerger management were better.

Virtually always, a merger/acquisition event starts out as a financial proposition. But once the papers have been signed, it becomes a human transaction. The way the human beings in the two companies behave will be the primary determinant of how well the financial gamble pays off.

Even the most astute dealmakers need to be followed by informed, capable managers. And the less skilled the dealmakers were to begin with, the more of a burden postmerger management has to bear.

THE COST OF LOST TALENT

Bailing out by managers and executives is one of the first signals that a merger is being mismanaged. Typically some of the best talent is the first to go. And their leaving more than likely means that somebody in the top ranks of the company made a mistake. There was something someone did, or didn't do, that helped produce the bailouts.

Parent company executives have to move fast and do the right things to keep the people who count. Too often, though, just the opposite happens. The acquiring firm drags its feet and does things clumsily.

In a 1982 article in *Chief Executive*, Robert E. Lamalie (president of the executive search firm, Lamalie Associates, Inc.) reports on a study his firm conducted of postacquisition executive turnover. He writes:

> In the cases of both hostile and friendly takeovers, 52 percent of executives had left the acquired company by the third year following the acquisition.[4]

Many factors contribute to the turnover statistics in mergers. People leave for myriad reasons—some that make sense, some

---

[4]Robert E. Lamalie, "What Happens to Executives after a Hostile Takeover," *Chief Executive*, Autumn 1982.

that don't. But the point is that many of these people are very valuable employees, and they could have been retained.

So what does the loss of talent cost a company?

First, there are some tangible, easily identifiable expenses associated with replacing a key manager or executive. Dr. Bradford D. Smart offers a pragmatic assessment of these in his excellent book, *Selection Interviewing* (see Figure 1).

The intangible costs associated with losing a key person are harder to gauge, although they can easily represent an even more expensive proposition than that shown in the chart below.

Usually a company not only loses some of its own talent but also ends up strengthening the competition. The most obvious place for a talented individual to go is to a competing firm where his or her skills are immediately transferable and actively sought.

There also are times when acquirers end up paying for people who aren't there. Mismanagement can frustrate and aggravate key players to the point that they decide to bail out and pull the cord on their golden parachutes. This is like the opposite of a

---

FIGURE 1

	$20,000 per Year Factory Supervisor	$50,000 per Year Sales Person	$100,000 per Year Technical Manager
Placement/search firm fees	$ —	$15,000	$ 30,000
Other recruitment/training costs (salaries of personnel people, training programs, air fares, motels, etc.)	1,000	10,000	25,000
Time of nonpersonnel people (other than hiring manager) in the selection process	1,000	4,500	10,000
Time wasted by hiring manager in the selection process and in training and managing the individual	3,000	10,000	20,000
Relocation costs	—	15,000	35,000
Total	$5,000	$54,500	$120,000

SOURCE: Bradford D. Smart, *Selection Interviewing* (New York: John Wiley & Sons, 1983) p. 4. © Copyright 1983 by John Wiley & Sons. Reprinted with permission of John Wiley & Sons.

signing bonus—top talent people basically pocket a big chunk of money and quit.

THE FINANCIAL DAMAGE OF LOST PRODUCTIVITY

Only a handful of senior people are likely to have such a ripcord to pull. Most people feel they have no good alternatives, so they stay and endure their frustrations. But the company can very easily end up paying for people who come to work but don't work.

When mergers are mismanaged, productivity never escapes unscathed. If a firm can quantify it, there will be disturbing financial evidence of how mismanagement carries a cost in terms of weaker productivity. The work hours that are lost without any meaningful output add up in a hurry.

When the merger is marked by weak leadership, poor communication, a lack of decision making, and so on, productivity takes a beating. As job commitment and employee morale weaken, less effort is put into the task at hand.

The merger impact studies conducted by my firm, Pritchett and Associates, Inc., indicate a minimum 15 percent loss in performance effectiveness among middle managers who are involved in the merger integration process. Senior executives have a much higher statistic.

These people very often will feel, and accurately so, that they are working harder than ever. But so much time, effort, and mental energy are being invested in merger-specific activity that the more basic business itself actually receives less true attention.

For a more specific calculation of the actual dollar cost to a company whose people are losing productive hours because the merger is being mismanaged, consider this example:

1. A newly acquired firm has 500 employees, with an average cost per work-hour of $28.
2. During the first eight months of the mergers, a conservative average of one work-hour per person is lost each day as a result of merger-produced problems–for example, confusion, gossiping, worrying, waiting for clear-cut directions and objectives, inability to get answers, trying to figure out new policies and procedures, privately conducting a job hunt over company telephones, etc.

3. One hour, times 500 employees, times $28 per hour, results in a $14,000 per day lost productivity cost to the company.
4. In a week, $70,000 has been spent in compensation that produced no constructive benefit for the company.
5. After just two months—another very conservative estimate for how prolonged merger integration periods tend to be—there has been a $560,000 loss to the company.

What does the firm have to generate in gross sales revenues to bring that amount of money to the bottom line? If it's operating at a 10 percent profit margin, it will take an extra $5.6 million in sales to offset this figure—at a time when overall corporate sales are more likely to be slipping than gaining.

Also, this does not take into consideration scrap or work that does get turned out and delivered although it is of poor quality, thus creating another set of future problems that carry a hefty cost as well.

THE PRICE TAG ON LOSS OF COMPETITIVE POSITION

A merger produces many distractions that cause employees to focus on themselves and the inner workings of the organization rather than on the marketplace. To put it differently, people take their eyes off the ball. Personal concern for their own careers is heightened, while concern for the company slips.

Companies that are being acquired and merged almost always have a difficult time maintaining their competitive edge. The more the integration process is mismanaged, the more the company is likely to lose existing marketshare or miss opportunities that come along to gain ground.

Soldiers who are poorly led show little determination. They are not aggressive. And when the corporate troops become preoccupied with themselves and demoralized about their work, they lose their fighting spirit. Sales drop off. Customer loyalty deteriorates. Competitors smell blood and rush in for the kill.

Competitive position can be ravaged when the integration phase is prolonged or poorly managed. How can that be translated into dollars and cents?

Tom Bligh, vice president of sales for CooperVision/CILCO of Seattle, gives a good example. He explains how, in his company's optical lens business, 1 percent of marketshare represents approximately 10,000 lenses. With a "per-lens" price that can be pegged around $300, a loss of 1 percent marketshare would translate into a loss of $3 million-per quarter. When asked how easy it is for a company in that particular industry to lose a percent of the market, Tom unhesitatingly replied, "Easy!"

But instead of just focusing on the negative possibilities, or on how mismanaged mergers can cause a loss of competitive position, one also needs to look at the upside potential. Tom Bligh reports that when only a few months into the merger of CooperVision and CILCO, the combined organization had achieved a 2 percent marketshare gain in its last quarter. So instead of a loss of $3 million, for example, management was able to gain 2 percent of marketshare and add $6 million in revenues.

If one looks at the dollar spread between successful and unsuccessful merger management, in this case there was a $9 million swing.

THE EXPENSE OF UNION PROBLEMS

The attitudinal climate and employee concerns manifested in the merger integration period represent a fertile breeding ground for unions.

It is a time during which employees feel unrepresented and vulnerable. They worry about losing seniority and some of their benefits. It strikes them as unfair that they have to adapt to the acquirer's policies and procedures. They grow frustrated with their inability to get answers, and feel they have no one they can safely turn to with their problems and complaints.

People, frequently at many different levels in the firm, talk about being "sold out" by the owners or the most senior executives. Frequently they look at the management contracts, golden parachutes, and special severance arrangements the top brass arrange for themselves and talk resentfully with each other about how the people in charge line their own pockets.

Employees witness major layoffs and feel they have little hope of success at defending their best career interests as individuals.

Psychologically, they seek safety and security. But their bosses, the people in the management ranks, generally are themselves stressed out to a large degree. Their work is demanding more of them, and they have their own personal interests to worry about.

So managers may do a poor job of offering nurturance and support. Typically they don't even do as good a job of communicating as they would under normal business conditions. Thus, rank-and-file employees may be quite receptive to union organizers who come by promising to take care of just the sort of problems the people are experiencing.

A bargaining unit offers ready refuge for people who are feeling "mergerized." They may not be so much pro-union as they are anti-management, or just willing to accept any port in a storm.

It is also possible that unionization will appeal to employees simply because of the revenge factor. Feeling victimized and unappreciated, they may look at voting in a union as one way of getting even with the company.

When people succumb to merger burnout and turn to a union in search of a higher degree of corporate advocacy, what does this cost the company?

It's interesting to see top executives start scrambling when they're confronted with a unionization threat. They get agitated because there is money at stake and because the job of managing a merger often gets even more complicated if a union gains entry.

One of the country's most highly regarded electrical utility companies was involved in an internal merger, a broad-scale restructuring that involved major consolidations and fundamental changes in the power structure. The usual merger dynamics were set in motion: a surge of ambiguity and uncertainty, a drop in the trust level, and self-protective behaviors on the part of employees. That in turn produced the customary organizational problems, as follows:

1. Communication difficulties.
2. A productivity sag.
3. Loss of team play.
4. Power struggles.
5. Low morale and weak commitment.
6. Bailing out.

Traditionally, the three subsidiary power companies within the holding company had conducted employee attitude and opinion surveys on a regular basis. But because of the organizational distress brought about by the merger, top management in the subsidiaries talked the situation over and concluded that the surveys should be postponed a year or so.

The reasoning? People were upset, the results would obviously be pretty negative, and more changes were forthcoming anyway, so why not "give things a chance to settle down." (Employees, by the way, were very disapproving of management's decision once word leaked out.)

Just a few weeks later, the news surfaced that a white-collar group of employees in one of the subsidiary companies was involved in an organizing effort. Top management panicked. The survey idea was quickly reconsidered, and data gathering for the survey began shortly thereafter. A senior manager remarked, "Our people don't feel represented in this environment, and I'm not sure they are; 175 people changed top management's mind overnight regarding this opinion survey."

Regrettably, it was too little, or it came too late, to stop the union from winning the election. So now management has a new headache, and labor has a new foothold.

The merger impact surveys conducted by my firm reveal that out of 14 different key factors likely to be affected by mergers, the most negatively impacted are (a) level of job stress and (b) overall morale.

The overall ranking of these factors by employees, from those items that are least negatively affected to those that are hit the hardest, is as follows (Figure 2):

FIGURE 2

1. Image in the business community.   } Positive Impact
2. Reaction of clients/customers.
3. Working relationships.
4. Company loyalty.
5. Job satisfaction.
6. Employee productivity.
7. Overall operating effectiveness.
8. Effectiveness of management/supervision.
9. Communications.   } Negative Impact
10. Problem solving and decision making.
11. Clarity of goals and objectives.
12. Clarity of guidelines/policies/procedures.
13. Morale.
14. Job stress.

THE COST OF MISCASTING PEOPLE

One of the most common results of mismanaged mergers is bad staffing decisions. And those decisions, in turn, contribute to further mismanagement as the integration process continues.

My earlier book, *After the Merger: Managing the Shockwaves* (Homewood, Ill.: Dow Jones-Irwin, 1985), takes a comprehensive look at the careless, unsystematic way staffing decisions typically are made when companies merge, and outlines the approach needed to prevent the expensive miscasting of people.

The way many companies, even big and supposedly sophisticated firms, approach the staffing issue is often indefensible. The decisions regarding who will go, who will stay, and who will go where, are made on the basis of expediency, favoritism, hunches, first impressions, highly questionable secondhand information, and negotiated trade-offs. The result, obviously, is that important management and executive slots are filled by misfits.

A man who is strong technically but doesn't have a nickel's worth of management aptitude or interpersonal skills is tapped to head up a research and development function. A highly structured, deliberate, slow-paced person is named to a vice president's job that involves vague assignments, requires a high tolerance for ambiguity, demands decisiveness, and desperately needs someone with a sense of urgency.

These people are going to fail. They are going to cost the company a lot of money and cause misery for others.

Why did they get these jobs in the first place?

The R&D fellow just happened to be in the wrong place (for the company, that is) at the right time. His boss, who would have been the obvious choice, and who could have done a good job, had joined a competing firm a few weeks before the merger. He had not been replaced. So the company made one of the common staffing mistakes: struggling to work with what you have instead of going after what you need.

The vice president ended up in his slot because the two merging companies were swapping jobs and people in a lame attempt to be fair and equitable—sort of like choosing up sides—and this fellow had to go somewhere.

Another basic casting mistake comes when companies give people "appeasement positions" that cripple effectiveness. This is particularly prone to happen when there are individual investors who want a title, seek power and status, yet have minimal talents to offer.

How do you go about telling a man who has just invested a chunk of his money, and who now owns 20 percent of the company, that he cannot be executive vice president or whatever.

The best way, by far, is to involve experts in staffing decisions and restructuring issues. They can bring objectivity plus a valuable background of experience that lets them speak authoritatively about things.

A good merger consultant will challenge faulty reasoning, and also can speak with frankness about someone's qualifications when a coinvestor might feel uncomfortable being so blunt. Let the consultant be the "heavy" and help broker the negotiations on sensitive staffing issues.

Miscasting of people can cost a great deal. It sometimes results in overstaffing, and that obviously means unnecessary names on the payroll. It may also result in understaffing, which can be just as costly or even more expensive.

The people who are going to carry major responsibility for managing the merger process need to possess several key characteristics:

> High energy level.
> Flexibility, and the ability to improvise.
> Decisiveness.
> Strong interpersonal skills.
> A willingness, and ability, to take charge.
> A knack for keeping many balls in the air simultaneously.
> A keen sense of urgency.
> High tolerance for stress and pressure; psychological
>   resilience.

These are characteristics that equip a person to manage transition and be an agent of change. If the right people are in charge, many problems will be prevented, and they will be able to cut the firm's losses on those that cannot be avoided.

COACHING POINTS

1. Spend money on prevention. Cures are much more expensive. Don't wait until you're forced into the position of having no alternative except damage control.

2. The most important thing to do well—really well—is to put the right people in the right places. Don't get sloppy on this one. And involve an outsider with an expert eye.

CHAPTER TWO

Getting in Touch with Merger Problems

The management corps in both the parent firm and the acquisition will commonly be seen doing a variety of things that really don't seem to make sense. To the casual observer, or to the person who is being directly affected, the leaders may appear foolish and inconsiderate. They may be accused of acting selfishly. Their actions may seem shortsighted and just plain dumb.

What's more, those may very well be accurate descriptions. But it is safe to say that the leaders in both firms are not deliberately ineffective, careless, or hardhearted in their efforts to manage the situation.

The odds are they will be giving it their best shot, based on how they see things and what they are trying to accomplish. To that extent, they usually deserve the benefit of the doubt.

Still, just because management is well intentioned does not mean it's making the right move. And if it's a wrong move, it doesn't really matter whether the rationale can be readily explained as being merely the result of faulty reasoning or misplaced priorities.

If it's wrong, it's wrong.

What, then, are some of the most common reactions of managers to merger problems, and how can they be explained? How do management teams foul up?

FAILURE TO RECOGNIZE PROBLEMS

Quite often managers and executives in the acquiring firm simply are not aware of the nature and extent of problems the merger creates in the acquisition.

Of course, that's not a legitimate excuse for letting the problems develop in the first place or, in the second place, not coming to grips with them in a timely manner. But while it does not justify anything, it does capture the reality of what happens: The leaders just lose touch with the organization.

A small electronics manufacturer in the Southwest was acquired by a large, diversified firm headquartered in the northeastern part of the United States. Very early in the merger the parent company assumed an adversarial stance and was highly confrontive in dealing with management of the smaller firm. The hardboiled manner of the acquirer, whether it came naturally or was deliberately designed to intimidate, had a devastating effect on the smaller organization. Some of the acquired firm's executives became unbelievably resistive and oppositional. Others became inhibited. Virtually everyone in the management ranks became angry, bitter, and demoralized.

The big question was which of the acquisition's top three executives would be the first to bail out. The second question was whether the parent company would succeed in keeping any of the management team intact—something that was badly needed.

As it turned out, the number-two man in the firm, an exceptionally capable young star, quit in disgust almost immediately. If he had stayed just a few days longer, there is little question that the president would have been the first to leave.

But the executive vice president preempted him. So the president felt compelled to grit his teeth, stay for a while, and try to look out for his people's interests. The number-three executive was still looking for other employment when the merger was over a year old.

But throughout the entire episode, parent company management seemed oblivious to the destructive effect it was having on the company in which it was investing.

Over lunch one day the president of the acquisition said, "The merger was final 10 months ago, and I'm just now coming up for air." He explained how the parent company's lack of sensitivity to the impact it was having on the acquisition had essentially shattered his self-confidence and sabotaged his executive effectiveness for months. The acquirer's lack of perceptiveness to the impact of the merger had brought the target company to the brink of disaster. And through it all the parent firm never really understood just how wretched things were for people in the acquired company.

In this case, part of the problem could have been that top management in the parent company was geographically too far removed to see what was happening. There were, after all, thousands of miles separating the two firms, and the acquisition was pretty small in the parent company's scheme of things. Still, millions of dollars and a couple of hundred business careers were at stake.

Executives in the parent company should have been expecting and looking for some fairly significant problems, because they are generally apparent on the heels of a merger.

But often parent company executives lose touch with the misery a merger brings to lower-level personnel, particularly in the acquired firm. The line of thinking seems to be, "I'm not hurting or worried, why should there be suffering down in the trenches?"

Even top managers in the acquisition, who have cut their own deal and therefore can rest easy, or who were very secure all along, just seem to have trouble understanding that there is so much stress and frustration among others.

But it's there. And so long as top management remains oblivious to the situation, the pain is prolonged and secondary problems can easily develop.

One of the country's largest insurance firms experienced significant merger problems in a Midwestern city where an acquisition's office was being merged. The executive there who ran the parent company's office prided himself on his open-door policy and his practice of "MBWA" (managing by wandering around). He was a perceptive man and a hands-on manager.

He readily agreed that the personnel in the local office of the firm being acquired were stressed out and showing a pronounced slump in morale. At the same time, though, he was quite convinced that the people in his own operation were accepting the idea of the merger and felt well informed. Thus, when it was suggested that he survey his employees to monitor reactions to the merger, he was fully cooperative, yet he saw it as a needless exercise.

The negative survey results stunned him. He immediately

called a meeting of all employees, held up the results and said in dismay, "Why didn't anybody tell me these things?"

Perhaps they did, and he simply didn't listen well or take them seriously. Most likely he was only given hints or innuendo, such that employees' anxiety and concerns went undetected by him.

But there he was, feeling that he hád his finger on the pulse of the merger when, in fact, he was unaware of the negative climate developing just a few feet outside his office door.

DISREGARD FOR PROBLEMS

Sometimes top management knows the merger/acquisition is not proceeding well in certain respects but chooses to turn its back on the problems. What could motivate this kind of behavior?

Well, the leaders may be preoccupied with other matters. That makes sense if the focus of attention is on deservedly higher priorities. But sometimes upper management just seems somewhat unconcerned, or not worried enough to take the situation seriously.

It may be a case of misplaced priorities. There are some firms that simply don't want to spend any money on the people problems a merger commonly creates. Rather, they accept the post-merger trauma as something that just goes with the territory, and are content to go on about their business assuming the problems will work themselves out as time goes by.

This is not a thrifty stance to take. It disregards the hidden economics of a merger, where the deal loses value through the loss of key talent, an alienated work force, and so on. The acquirer that doesn't pay now (taking the needed "preventive management" steps) will inevitably pay later.

In some instances the acquirer ignores many of the management and human resource problems of mergers because nobody in the top management circle has a real good idea of how the troublesome issues should be addressed. Faced with not knowing many of the right things to do, they don't do much of anything, except hope the problems will go away.

That's high-risk management, though, because a head-in-the-sand approach can just as easily lead to problems that grow worse with the passing of time. It makes much more sense to call in professional help.

The ignoring approach also is frequently preferred by executives and managers who see the merger problems quite clearly but feel like it would be dangerous to acknowledge or admit them. The reasoning process here is to "let sleeping dogs lie." Privately, top management will agree that problems exist, but then go on to say that nothing directly will be done to deal with the situation.

The explanation? Well, top management won't explain it this way, but what it comes down to is that management is afraid that in acknowledging the problems and seeking to address them openly, they would more or less "legitimize" peoples' discontent, complaints, and so forth. Management is reluctant to do or say anything that might confirm the fears or frustrations.

As a result, merger transition problems go unattended.

DENIAL OF PROBLEMS

The management headaches and people problems that are so basic, so generic, to mergers are often met with strong denial by parent company executives. Problems begin to surface on a variety of fronts. People gripe, complain, and ventilate their frustrations, while top management stonewalls it.

This is quite different from the two previous reactions. Here, management is not oblivious to the problems but simply refuses to acknowledge them in the proper light. And it's not the same as ignoring the things that are going wrong—rather, it amounts to denying that there are real problems by minimizing them or trying to rationalize them away.

So the scenario goes something like this: Employees come forth to express their fears, and top management dismisses them with the words, "You don't have anything to worry about."

The common theme of company gossip relates to merger problems and how the organization is coming apart at the seams. But top management sends out the empty reassurances, "We're already past the worst part," or "Things really aren't as bad as you think," or "It's not happening here . . . it's not that bad in our company."

Of course, the words don't sell. Employees throughout the organization know what they see and they know how they feel.

And what they see and feel just is not consistent with the rhetoric of upper-level executives.

Consultants can understand how frustrating this must feel to the employee because, as outsiders, they sometimes run into the same dilemma in trying to get the attention of top management.

Consultants occasionally sit down with upper-level executives to communicate (1) how stressed out employees are and (2) how the frustration level is as high as morale is low. Too often executives simply will not come to grips with the reality of what is being reported. Instead, their response—while it's worded differently—amounts to, "There may be a few minor problems here and there, but that's to be expected."

When the consultant proceeds to describe operating tangles and productivity problems that are developing, sometimes the executives respond, "People haven't let on to me that there are serious problems . . . so there must not really be anything wrong. I think you're exaggerating."

These responses are a sure sign that management is beginning to distance itself from the reality of the work force. It's a communication problem that has costly ramifications.

Some of the denial undoubtedly results from the fact that top management, usually in both companies, has a strong vested interest in making the merger work. They have to "promote it," or "sell it," to the work force.

It is sort of like a man and a woman, both with children from an earlier marriage, who decide they are in love and want to remarry. They may be all for it, but that doesn't mean their kids are. The kids will decide for themselves whether it's a good marriage or a bad one. They won't pay much attention to what the parents say about the merging of the two families. What matters to them is how they personally feel, how they are affected. And what they experience may cause them to describe the new family situation as a miserable mess that isn't working well at all. But if the parents don't pay attention, if they fail to respond, the kids will basically write them off and then fight back through a variety of maladaptive behaviors.

Employees do the same sort of thing in the merger environment. If management won't listen and get interested in the problems, employees take matters into their own hands. They will find their own "solutions." People just further discredit what management says and typically (a) give up, (b) get even, or (c) go off in their own direction. Then one day managers look around and realize the organization isn't lined up behind them.

It reminds me of a quote I saw on a wall plaque in a client's office one day:

I must hurry. They have gone, and I am their leader.

It's an easy trap for top executives to get caught up in the same propaganda they are feeding to the employees. It's sort of like beginning to believe their own press releases while refusing to acknowledge disconcerting data bubbling up from the lower ranks of the organization.

But just denying that problems are there doesn't make them go away. It just means top management has decided to warp the reality of what's going on.

The treacherous part of all this is that so often top management (maybe just in the parent company, but sometimes in both firms) honestly believes the merger is under control, that it's being well managed, and that enough is being done to carry the companies through the transition period satisfactorily. Plus, there is a tendency to pooh-pooh many of the criticisms and complaints that are heard as being "the normal griping you can expect from some people."

Naturally, as long as this viewpoint prevails, it's hard to get executives interested in changing their game plan. Merger problems often get out of hand before they are taken seriously. Even then, top management's response is commonly too little too late.

Just as husbands and wives with marital problems are often reluctant to seek professional counseling, executives sometimes dislike the idea of turning to a consultant for help with corporate marriage problems. Typically managers feel they should be able to work things out on their own, that they shouldn't have to bring in outside expertise.

It may be embarrassing to let an outsider see how rotten things are. Or, like in a regular marriage where only one of the couple is doing the "suffering," a top executive may not be feeling enough of the pain to recognize the need for intervention by a management consultant who understands mergers and can get at the truth. At any rate, it is well known that marriages are usually on the rocks before people turn to the professionals, and by then the relationship may be damaged beyond repair.

The point that will be made repeatedly, and hopefully driven home, is that there will invariably be a new set of management problems that develop as a result of a company's being merged or acquired. That's inescapable.

Hopefully there also will be enthusiasm and a sense of optimism that develop about the future. Plus, if things are managed adroitly, there is every reason to believe that management can use the merger to achieve new levels of employee motivation and productivity.

But the beneficial results can be long delayed or made impossible if top management denies, ignores, or is oblivious to the organizational problems a merger brings.

THE MANAGEMENT HOT SEAT

To understand the situation better, keep in mind that top management in the acquired firm wants to look good to the parent company.

Those executives feel they are being graded (and they are!). Understandably, acquired company executives don't like to come forth and tell the acquirer that something is not working in the merger. They don't like to have to step forward and complain or report organizational breakdowns. This carries a large amount of risk.

Top executives in the acquisition normally have a new place in the pecking order as a result of being acquired and merged. They're positioned with a new set of superiors, new bosses, and they are in the process of having to earn their spurs or prove themselves again. So there is a tendency on their part not to want to wrestle with problems that carry a high potential for failure. They don't want to even face up to them, much less go looking for such trouble.

Merger problems that develop create a dilemma and put management in a bind. Such problems threaten the managers' and executives' reputations as well as their new relationships with the parent company.

As a result, acquired company leaders usually do not want to carry the problems to parent company management. To begin with, they may feel they will be blamed for the fact that the problems exist. There is the fear that they will be nailed for being ineffective in the way they are managing the merger and not keeping things on an even keel.

Executives also worry that if they point out merger problems that are developing, they will be accused of being resistive to the merger. And since they don't want to be blamed for causing the problems or mishandling them, they simply choose not to bring up the subject of what's going wrong.

The acquirer must be very careful not to throw any of the following responses at people who step forth to report merger problems. Here are four ways to go about "shooting the messenger":

1.   *"You're wrong. There are no significant problems."*

     This sort of response basically communicates that the messenger is viewed to be dumb, imperceptive, or guilty of blowing things out of proportion.

     It's worth remembering that employees who report problems feel their claims are legitimate. At least from where they sit, something is wrong and needs the attention of higher management. If superiors don't take the words to heart, why should subordinates be expected to keep coming forth with their complaints?

     And you can bet on it, sooner or later things that higher management would agree are significant concerns will end up not being reported.

2.   *"If there are problems, they are your fault."*

     The parent company should be determined to stay current about problems or potential problems, and not be preoccupied with assigning blame. People who have the guts to report problems position themselves to receive help, and that should work to both companies' advantage.

     Employees who get hammered and blamed when they announce something is going wrong soon learn to hide mistakes and problems. Individual survival in the corporate jungle depends on doing what works best. If it doesn't work when employees flag problems and ask for help, they won't do it for long.

3.   *"You're being resistive. You're a troublemaker. You had better get on board."*

     Too often managers and executives, especially in the

parent company, equate the reporting of problems with being resistive. Anyone who doesn't parrot the party line that "This is a good merger, everything's fine and dandy" and so on, gets accused of being an insurgent or foot-dragger. People get the message in a hurry—don't tell the truth, tell them what they want to hear.

Why can't parent company executives appreciate the reality that, in fact, one of the slickest and safest ways to be *truly* resistive is to stand by quietly and watch problems develop?

If you accuse people of being resistive and causing trouble just because they point out merger problems, you train them to be silent saboteurs.

4. *"Okay, you say there is a problem, go take care of it. Fix it."*

Here the messenger walks away realizing that reporting problems just makes life more complicated. No new resources are provided to deal with the difficulties, but the responsibility for correcting the situation has been dumped on the poor soul who called attention to it. There is a new level of accountability, but no real backing from higher management.

Again, people catch on quickly. They learn to keep their mouths shut, take the line of least resistance, and not assume any responsibility for merger foul-ups.

So, as it turns out, parent company management (and often senior management in the acquisition) frequently doesn't get a true reading on how the merger is working for people in the acquired firm. Word gets around quickly that this is a company that shoots messengers who carry bad news.

Executives get an edited, sanitized version that people in the acquisition feel is "acceptable," "safe," or "what parent company management wants to hear." The nature of the problems may be disguised, the extent of the problems watered down or glossed over.

It seems that the higher one is on the corporate ladder in the acquisition, the more reluctance there is to be a bearer of bad news or to ask for help.

But remember, this may be the first time in many years that executives in the acquisition have had to really answer to a higher ranking person in the corporate chain of command. They may be very unaccustomed to being closely observed and evaluated. They will wonder how the new boss keeps score. It usually creates some discomfort, and will probably lead to some self-protective behavior. Acquired company executives will follow whatever routes they usually do in those conditions where they are being evaluated as individuals—and often some of those behaviors are dysfunctional.

It's not uncommon for key executives in the acquisition to take a hard look at themselves and question their abilities during the merger transition period.

But it goes well beyond that.

These executives also know that they are being evaluated both from above (by the parent company) and from below (by their own employees, who are wondering if the boss can measure up to this new test and whether he or she will look out for his or her subordinates' interests satisfactorily).

Half of that evaluation the upper executives are not familiar with—that from the acquirer. And the other half, that from subordinates, is something the boss has not really had to worry much about in the first place. Previously the "old man" could more or less deal with that in his own way, because he was at the top of the ladder. But in the merger environment, he begins to worry about how he is being "voted on" by people above as well as below him. He begins to "lobby" and try to sell everybody on the idea of his effectiveness.

It's important to understand the pressure points that affect the top executives in the acquisition. The acquisition's top officer, in particular, must attend to both camps of evaluators.

The people that are both higher and lower in the chain of command have to be convinced that everything is cool, that the boss has it under control, that the merger is not too big for him to handle. So he can easily fall into the trap of minimizing problems.

When this begins to happen, and lower-level people feel that their cries for help are not being heard, management begins to lose credibility. Top executives run a real risk when they turn a deaf ear or otherwise discount the lamentations of middle managers or the rank and file.

Senior executives, especially those primarily responsible for putting the deal together, feel compelled to declare that the merger *will* work—that it *is*, in fact, working. But when employees disagree, and promptly offer firsthand evidence of where they see it balling up, the people at the top had better listen.

It is here, though, that upper-level executives often make the wrong choice. Upon getting wind of the management headaches and personnel problems that are developing at various points in the acquisition (or perhaps in both companies, if a true merger is being sought), key executives' responses often amount to insisting, "It's gonna work, it's gonna work . . . overall things are looking real good," and so on.

Of course, the people who are struggling aren't persuaded at all. They just become more aggravated with their leaders, more frustrated with the merger, and less willing to point out problems that truly do call for top management intervention.

These lower-level people may very well throw up their hands, concluding that it's futile to try and turn the ear of anyone high enough in the organization to correct the situation. Thus, basic problems fester, secondary problems develop, and employee morale and motivation go south.

The better choice is for top management to listen, really hear people out, and take the message seriously. Instead of denying problems and disliking critics, they would do well to emulate Charles F. Kettering, who said, "Problems are the price of progress. Don't bring me anything but trouble."

As merger problems are identified and called to the attention of the key leaders, their responses should be, "That's important. Now let's get into that. What do you see? Where do you see it not working? What do you see as being a problem? What needs to happen?"

This sends a very potent message to people. It demonstrates that management wants to know about problems, about merger breakdowns. It lets employees feel safe about bringing bad news.

Management should consider the possibility that the intervention point where recruitment of employee commitment is most promising will very likely be precisely where people are disagreeing with the fact that the merger is working.

This may seem very paradoxical to key leaders—for example, that the places they need to explore are those areas where, clearly, people are disagreeing with the fact that the merger is going well. Top management has to look for the contradictions to the merger working. That has to be the key point of focus, the main point of inquiry.

How the leaders handle this—the behavior they model—sends heavy-duty messages to the people throughout the acquisition.

ACTION VERSUS WORDS

Talk is cheap. Employees don't want verbal reassurance or promises that have a hollow ring. What management *says* counts for little; what management *does* is everything.

Corporate growth through mergers and acquisitions calls for action-oriented management, for executives who will find and then face up to the problems and aggravations that routinely occur when the attempt is being made to buy and blend organizations.

But, of course, just being action oriented is not enough. The steps that are taken have to be the right ones, and in the merger environment that is not as easy as it looks.

Frequently executives take very well-intentioned steps that are dead wrong. Then, too, there are instances where the right steps, taken too slowly, or too quickly, become the wrong ones because the timing is off. Chapter Three will go into detail in explaining the most common mistakes in postmerger management.

COACHING POINTS

1.   Expect problems. To do otherwise is to kid yourself. They will be out there . . . somewhere. Be mentally prepared for merger shockwaves. If you're not aware of any problems, that is a problem in itself. Get in touch with your organization.

2.   Go looking for trouble. Sniff it out. Magnetize yourself to bad news. You need to know what you are up against. You can't lead if you are one of the last to know. You can't come to grips with problems when you are oblivious to them.

3.   Reward people who identify problems and report breakdowns. Don't shoot messengers. Make it clear that the truth is welcome. Diagnosis is the first step toward treatment. Deputize every employee. Do not automatically accuse them of being complainers or being resistive.

4.   Belly up to bad news. Don't try to downplay problems or manipulate reality. If your people say there is a problem, take it seriously. They see things you can't see, and they look at the things you can see in a different light than you do. Their perspective may be better than yours. At the very least, their viewpoint is important to them and thus should be important to you.

5.   When people flag problems, enlist their help in finding solutions. The odds are they will be one of your best resources. But don't just throw the problem back at them with instructions to "fix it." Provide—through yourself or others—assistance in analyzing and understanding the situation. Help them identify and obtain the resources needed to deal with it. But be sure to keep them involved in the effort to take care of the matter. Involvement enhances their commitment to solving the problem, and their ownership of the problem-solving approach. Also, when people have to struggle with problems, they are more accepting of solutions that are less than perfect.

6.   Move on problems. Prevention is best, but second best is nipping problems in the bud. It is usually much easier to come to grips with difficulties when you address them early on. Problems that are ignored tend to become bigger, often creating secondary problems as well. Don't drag your feet. Role model a sense of urgency for all to follow.

Avoiding the Most Common Management Mistakes

Mergers call for flexible management. The ability to improvise, to adjust quickly to changing circumstances, is a critical skill. Also, management must be prepared to make some "counterintuitive moves," addressing situations and tackling problems in ways that run counter to what seems on the surface to be a sensible, obvious way of dealing with things.

Organizations involved in significant transition and change cannot be managed effectively with the same routines, perspectives, and priorities that work when one is merely managing the status quo.

Mergers generate too many pressure points for that. The emotional climate is too highly charged. The pace of change accelerates too much, and the time window for doing certain things is too narrow to allow for much error in the staging of certain actions.

Managers and executives need to switch gears in order to maneuver around some very common management mistakes that occur during the merger integration process.

VIOLATION OF EXPECTATIONS

This managerial error usually shows up very early in the merger/acquisition scenario. Basically it is a credibility problem that plagues management.

First Announcements. The initial groundwork is laid for violating expectations when a top executive makes the formal announcement that a firm is being acquired or merged. Often the press release hits the high points of the merger, goes into a little more detail on a couple of issues, then delivers the standard party line in a quote from a ranking officer:

> No changes in management are anticipated. The acquisition will basically continue to operate as it has in the past.

Then, to rule out any possibility that this might later be blamed on lousy reporting, a representative of the parent company comes before employees in the acquisition to reiterate the same ideas face-to-face.

People in the acquired firm don't really believe it. Oh, a few of the more naive souls may accept it on faith, but most of the audience remain cynical and doubting. The irony, though, is that as the merger unfolds and the changes inevitably occur, virtually everyone in the acquisition will refer to top management's earlier statements as hard proof that the parent company has reneged on its promises.

First announcements about the merger are delicate messages. And giving people the impression that life will go on as usual is like walking into a management trap that has steel jaws.

There should be change. There will be change. And people know it.

One of the most constructive things top management can do is to get the complete story out about the merger as quickly as possible. The message should carefully detail plans for the combined operations and set forth goals, policies, and reporting relationships.

Because the first announcements are so crucial, they should be painstakingly crafted—bearing in mind that even under the best of circumstances, such public statements are often taken with a grain of salt.

Some Good News and Some Bad News. Hyping the merger is another seductive trap. Here again management creates unrealistic expectations, then violates them.

It must be remembered that the trust level is a fragile thing in merging companies. It is seriously threatened by the insecurities people are feeling. Sweeping statements designed to placate and reassure employees generally just add to the erosion of faith in what management says.

Skepticism makes people wary. They search for evidence that contradicts what they are being told, and they frequently find it. Some will conclude that they have been deliberately misled. Others will view it as an honest mistake, yet they too will weigh more dubiously any subsequent pronouncements from on high.

Managers and executives best protect their credibility when they prepare people for the worst—not like prophets of doom, but like realists.

It's an issue of leveling with the people. It's a management philosophy of "no surprises."

Top management must remember it is dealing with adults— people who are trying to earn a living, build a career, raise a family. It doesn't pay to sugar-coat the facts.

Neither should management just throw people a sales pitch about the positive side of the merger and all the promise it holds. Employees should be given a balanced viewpoint. It's a good news/bad news issue, where both sides of the story should be told.

The people can handle it. They deserve to know. And top management can't fool them for long anyway.

One might succeed in creating some false hope by focusing strictly on the good news, and maybe that buys the company some time. But it carries a hefty price tag, because as people's hope plays out, so does management's credibility. And when employees' hope and management's credibility fade, they will be replaced with resistance, lower morale, and cynicism.

It's astute management to let people know what they can expect. Give it to them straight. They will respect the company for it, and they'll also be better prepared psychologically to cope with frustrating or undesirable events if (or rather, when) they do occur.

If the company gets lucky and things happen to go better than was predicted, top management may even be seen as heroes. At least employees won't resent that turn of events, and the trust level will have been preserved.

Promises, Promises. The third management trap that leads to a violation of expectations is sprung when management grows careless in making commitments.

Employees will constantly push the boss to take a firm stand or give definite answers. But making promises is like playing with live ammunition. So often a middle manager or senior executive will go on the line and make a firm commitment, only to have it blow up in his face. Again, about the only safe promise is that there will be changes.

The problem of violated expectations, and the associated loss of management credibility, can be defended against by preparing employees for changes in the game plan. It is best to assure them that management will change its mind—on some things voluntarily, on others because circumstances will require it.

People should be told up front that some things that are done will be reworked or redone. The work force should be assured that the merger will inevitably involve some false starts and that management occasionally will have to back up and shift direction.

Why not lay it on the line and tell people that there are no "school solutions" to mergers, that instead there is much trial and error involved? It should be explained to employees that a lot of merger management is impromptu and that the people in charge have to improvise and feel their way along as the situation unfolds.

The Elusive Truth. A merger is like a fast-breaking story. Managers generally try to keep employees up-to-date on what's going on and what's planned, at least in the early stages of a merger. But the "facts" keep changing. Sometimes the truth is DOA (dead on arrival).

What often happens is that the boss reports the available news. Then fresh information comes along, or there are new developments, and the story changes. Sometimes rank-and-file people find out about it before their superior does. Then employees accuse management of misleading them, or lying, and the boss decides it's not safe to say much of anything. So a communication vacuum develops, and it's partly the fault of the employees themselves.

Communications are a chronic problem during the merger integration period. It makes a real difference, however, when people are told about this problem before the fact. It helps preserve managerial credibility and minimizes the problem of violated expectations.

The Cultural Imperative. A firm's corporate culture causes employees to operate with a certain set of assumptions and implicit expectations. The existing norms, beliefs, and values in the acquired firm, for example, are part of an unwritten but very important "psychological contract" between the employee and the employer.

There may be ingrained customs or rituals that people consider inviolable. When the acquirer treads on these, even inadvertently, employees often cry "foul"—especially if they were promised "no changes."

Corporate culture causes people to assume some rather crazy things about such issues as what's fair and unfair, how business should be conducted, who promotions should go to, or how differences are to be handled.

When these latent expectations are not met by the parent company in the merger, employees may accuse top management of treachery. And when people feel they've been treated unfairly, they generally retaliate in some fashion, even if covertly and attitudinally. Furthermore, they feel justified in doing so.

This highlights the need for top management to make a concerted effort toward helping people in the two companies reconcile their cultural disparities as soon as possible.

COACHING POINTS

1. Life is easier, for everybody, when management gets people emotionally prepared for change. Tell people "it ain't gonna be business as usual." That's a promise you can keep.

2. Don't give up on communicating. The tendency is for managers and executives to grow more cautious. They become more wary of going out on any kind of limb to pass along information, to tell people what to expect, or to make commitments. But managers need to communicate more, not less.

3. Don't lie. Don't dodge. Don't shave the truth.

4. Don't lead people to expect something you can't deliver. It is very easy to get into those boxes, and hard to get out of them.

5. Be up-front with bad news. Bold announcements are generally better than living with leaks, rumors, or the wild speculation of employees. So don't hedge. Don't deny problems or discount them. That easily creates false hope that is later dashed on the rocks of reality. Fancy footwork may enable management to duck issues for now, only to add to the distrust later.

6. Be big enough to admit mistakes—it gives amazing mileage to one's credibility and integrity. Also it gives others the courage to follow one's lead.

7. Explain things better. Managers should bring employees into their confidence. When telling people what's going to happen, take time to explain the rationale. Seriously consider letting them know what the options are. Generate some dialogue with them in those situations where it's not too late for them to suggest options and discuss alternatives. People normally handle things better when they understand the situation.

8. When something is taken away from employees, try to replace it with something else. Give people the sense that their interests have been respected, and that superiors have negotiated fairly for them. Help people to feel that an exchange has taken place, instead of their merely having lost something.

CRISIS OF LEADERSHIP

Most organizations are managed rather than led. This is a common problem in business, but the problem gets compounded in merging organizations.

The broad array of changes experienced by merging firms destabilizes corporate life. The resulting confusion and stress call for leadership. The change also creates an opening for leadership. Managers need to realize that this can be their finest hour. Simultaneously with this growing need for high caliber leaders, though, the amount and quality of leaderlike behavior diminishes.

Invariably there is some shuffling of people, with managers being recast in key roles. But sometimes that activity itself becomes part of the problem instead of part of the solution.

What Is Leadership? Putting a man in charge and calling him the leader is like giving a man a Bible and calling him a preacher. Bestowing the title doesn't bestow the talent.

In their outstanding book, *Leaders*, Warren Bennis and Burt Nanus submit, "Managers are people who do things right and leaders are people who do the right thing."[1]

Most managers in merging organizations seem to be very busy. Certainly a lot of energy is being burned up (albeit much of it by personal stress and unproductive pursuits). What's missing, though, are managers doing the *right things*.

Quite frankly, there is a crisis of leadership: "Leaders" are not leading. As a result, too much of the work force behaves like an unled army.

How the person in charge behaves is a critical matter. It's easy to make someone the boss. But you can't make that person a leader. And if he or she is not a leader, you often don't get followers.

The tendency is for top executives, middle managers, and lower-level supervisors to blame their lack of leadership on the situation, or on "higher management." Merger successes or corporate achievements, interestingly enough, are things for which they readily accept personal ownership. But as someone has said, "If you're going to take credit for the rain, don't be surprised when people blame you for the drought."

People at each level in the management hierarchy can rest assured that some of the criticism will be directed at them when lower-level employees critique the leadership situation in the merger and discuss how their own boss is functioning.

The question is, "What kills leadership?" What gets in the way?

Leadership gets killed through self-inflicted wounds. It's like this: I can't destroy *your* leadership ability, but I can kill mine.

The reverse is also true. If your effectiveness as a leader leaves much to be desired, rest assured, *you* are the one to blame.

Here are the things that do the major damage to leadership effectiveness:

---

[1]Warren Bennis and Burt Nanus, *Leaders* (New York: Harper & Row, 1985), p. 21.

1. Worrying about self.
2. Lack of purpose.
3. Lack of courage.
4. Weak commitment.
5. Loss of trust.

Certainly there are many other factors that can get in the way of one's leadership effectiveness, just as there are many things not implied in the list above that can enhance one's performance at leading. But these five items are so fundamental that they deserve special consideration.

1. *Worrying about Self.* A preoccupation with one's self interferes with (a) the needed goal orientation and (b) attention to the needs of those who are to be led.

Powerful leaders, on the other hand, seem to lose themselves in what they are doing. They are invested in a cause, and in others, rather than in the narcissistic exercise of focusing on themselves.

Sure, self-knowledge is essential. Introspection serves a purpose. But when a person spends too much time in front of the mirror, so to speak, the tasks of leadership go unattended.

Worrying about self also has an inhibiting influence on one's performance. For example, the athlete who is self-conscious typically tightens up and loses that fluid motion that produces the best results.

Mergers energize the self-preservation motive in managers. They worry more about "ol' number one," and give less attention to that part of the corporate army they're supposed to be leading. Also, their concern for themselves distracts them from the objectives.

2. *Lack of Purpose.* True leaders are people who operate with a clear sense of direction. They have a purpose, a "magnificent obsession."

It is this sense of vision that makes compelling leaders. Vision enables employees to follow, because it represents an aiming point for behavior. It "encourages" people, restoring some of the self-confidence that has ordinarily been shaken by merger events.

Any executive, manager, or supervisor is free to operate with vision, whether or not superiors have communicated an organization-wide cause or purpose. Ideally there will be a global vision serving the total company, but the people in charge at the various levels cannot afford to wait indefinitely for that to be forthcoming.

The clearer the vision's trumpet call, the better. A halting, off-key, indistinct message to "charge" doesn't muster much confidence or a fighting spirit in the troops. In fact, uncertainty at the top usually creates resistance lower down in the organization.

When companies are being acquired and merged, goals and objectives get blurry. People find it hard to lead because they don't know where the parent company wants them to go. So the organization as a whole, or certain key parts of it, wander and drift.

The situation calls to mind a movie from the 1960s, titled *Paint Your Wagon*. The story is about the mines playing out in a frontier gold rush town. Toward the end of the movie people are giving up and pulling out. The main actor, Lee Marvin, sits at the edge of town with his grizzled sidekick, watching the exodus of mules, wagons, and people heading out of town in a muddy procession toward the West. The sidekick looks at Lee Marvin and says, "I guess there are two kinds of people in the world—them that move, and them that stay. Ain't that the truth?" Lee Marvin just stares straight ahead and slowly growls, "No, that ain't the truth. Everybody's goin'. The only difference is, them goin' somewhere, and them goin' nowhere."

Leaders are going somewhere, somewhere in particular. And their vision inspires others to follow.

3. *Lack of Courage.* Leadership, sooner or later, requires a show of courage. There must be a willingness to take risks, to face the possibility of failure.

Strong leaders look at failure as part of the learning process, as something that provides data regarding the reorienting and fine-tuning that are needed to continue toward the desired vision.

But an analysis of merger behavior shows a large percentage of managers moving toward the sidelines, electing to minimize risk taking. Caution and conservatism seem to crowd out guts.

A chronic problem is for managers and executives to give

away their power. They feel impotent, and fail to test some of the assumptions they make regarding the limits of their ability to make decisions and take action. They disempower themselves, then blame higher management for causing the problem.

Mergers are a time for individual managers and executives to operate from the premise that it's easier to get forgiveness than permission. If one waits for highly definitive statements regarding what's okay, what the limits of authority are, and so forth, leadership effectiveness stalls out.

When firms are being merged and integrated, leadership effectiveness is more likely to be sabotaged by sins of omission rather than sins of commission.

Managers need to guard against moving into a play-it-safe stance. The tendency to do nothing rather than to do wrong produces widespread corporate inertia. Managers take a wait-and-see attitude, electing not to take risks until they have time to figure out how the "scorekeeping system" may have changed.

Let's face it—managers who are being acquired and merged face some tough questions:

1. Who's keeping score?
2. Whom do I need to please?
3. What's the new measuring stick?
4. How do you make points in this scorebook?

Management needs to move aggressively in answering these questions to everyone's satisfaction. Also, the people in charge must communicate that mistakes and errors are permissible in the postmerger environment. Performance should not have to be perfect.

The key to minimizing the inertia and postmerger drift lies in keeping people mobile and action oriented. Decision making should be encouraged. Risk taking should be reinforced, all in a spirit of conducting business competitively. Otherwise, people are going to lose their nerve. Their mistakes will be the ones borne of caution, lack of courage, and self-preservation instincts.

These sins of omission are insidious. They sneak up on you. Sometimes the damage they do goes unnoticed, or is almost impossible to calculate. But they are costly mistakes, and they also weaken one's effectiveness as a leader.

4. *Weak Commitment.* A person's staying power is determined by his or her level of commitment. It is commitment that energizes persistence.

Leaders are passionate people in their commitment. It is constancy that helps them command the confidence, respect, and overall backing of those who follow.

Persistence is 10 times more important than talent. That's because 9 times out of 10, talent comes out of persistence.

But the troublesome dynamics of mergers tend to produce decommitment. And as that happens, leadership receives another wound. Subordinates instinctively know when the boss' intensity begins to wane. The heat of their passion and commitment is, to a large degree, drawn from the leader's flame. When it begins to flicker, the drive of the entire group begins to cool off.

5. *Loss of Trust.* When trust is lost in the relationship between superiors and subordinates, leadership is dealt a near-fatal blow.

One can still function as a boss or manager. Orders can be given and obeyed, work assigned and completed, responsibilities delegated and carried out successfully. But that extra dimension of leadership that is so essential in times of transition and change has trust as its lifeblood.

Bennis and Nanus have described trust as "the emotional glue that binds followers and leaders together."[2] Trust is reciprocal—if you want employees to trust in you, it is necessary for you to trust in them. Managers have to weave the fine fabric of trust into the relationship with their people before they can truly function as leaders.

We should look at the word *manager* as a title or label, while *leadership* is a reputation. Reputations must be built. Earned. They must be protected, too, as months and years of constructive building of trust can be demolished in a matter of minutes when one behaves in an untrustworthy way.

Other Leadership Issues. In addition to the self-inflicted blows to leadership effectiveness, there are several practical aspects of mergers that contribute to the problem.

---

[2]Ibid., p. 153.

One reason mergers create a crisis of leadership, for example, is that ordinarily some of the best leaders in a company leave the scene. It is the strong swimmers who are the first to jump ship.

They usually have the most options. They are being actively recruited. Plus, their level of confidence and personal initiative gives them the nerve needed to shape their own careers.

A poorly defined chain of command also complicates the leadership process, as do the power struggles that invariably develop.

Even top management's preoccupation with putting the merger deal together is a distraction. The more executive time and effort expended in fighting the acquisition, trying to sell the company, or working on the merger agreement, the less time there is left to lead people.

Another problem is that there are managers and executives who fully intend to leave because of the merger, but they have to pick their timing carefully. Perhaps they have to remain for a few months in order to collect their profit sharing or year-end bonus. It may take them several weeks or months to carry out their job search. So they have to stay on for a while, but their heart is not in it.

They remain in a leadership position but they aren't leading. Further, they can't really pump up their people and demonstrate commitment because they've got integrity, and it would be difficult to enthusiastically live out a lie. As a result, they model a lack of commitment.

Finally, there is an interesting phenomenon that might be labeled the "sun and ski syndrome" that frequently interferes with postmerger leadership. In this scenario senior executives cut their own private deal with the acquiring company. Sometimes it amounts to a management contract. On other occasions it is a matter of their getting early closure regarding what their job title and responsibilities will be. Anyway, very quickly they get their personal situation squared away. The heat is off. The ambiguity is eliminated.

So what do they do? They leave, for one or two or maybe even four weeks, and take a breather. Some go skiing in Vail, others go to the Bahamas and get a suntan.

Meanwhile, their employees feel abandoned, and this is happening at the very time subordinates have the highest need for nurturing, support, and real leadership.

The following guidelines can help alleviate the crisis of leadership:

COACHING POINTS

1. Choose people carefully for leadership roles. Find people who want to lead and who can lead.

2. Sometimes the people in charge seem to go into hiding, when high visibility is what is needed. Managers should show a strong physical presence. Employees want to see, hear—even touch—the boss, particularly if he or she is new to the organization.

3. Determine what the chain of command will be, and communicate the lines of authority—do this as rapidly as you can do it in an informed manner. Managers left with ambiguous decision-making latitude often don't really know where and how much they can lead. So they stumble along waiting for clarification.

4. Develop a mission statement. A compelling purpose needs to be specified, one that people can support and get excited about pursuing. It can provide for the integration and channeling of energy. It is a key reference point in the midst of chaos.

5. Encourage managers to remain action oriented and willing to take risks. Permit mistakes. Reinforce action and decisiveness.

6. Take steps to either (a) create management commitment to the merger, or (b) restaff with key people who will personally "get on board," and who can rally the troops and generate loyalty/commitment.

7. Work hard to protect and/or restore trust.

8. Pass out the picture, and the story (background information), of any new management people.

MOVING TOO SLOWLY

Well-intentioned acquirers often opt for a merger integration strategy that involves a rather slow, measured pace in making changes. The logic influencing executives to proceed in this fashion appears sound, but is deceiving.

The rationale, as explained by executives, is that too much change, coming too quickly, could be overwhelming for employees.

They conclude that it would be better to make incremental changes in a deliberate, carefully staged fashion, allowing time for a dose of change to be assimilated before administering another.

But instead of worrying about having people "OD" on change, the primary concern should be to finish the merger and put an end to the suffering. It's the uncertainty and ambiguity that create the most stress—not knowing what will happen, when it will happen, or how one will be affected. The longer these issues go unanswered, the more merging firms are likely to lose productivity, as well as their people.

Human beings can handle a high level of change. They adjust and adapt remarkably well—if there is something solid they can adjust to.

But people have an uncanny, intuitive feel for when the transition and change of a merger is actually over. Certainly they are savvy and perceptive enough not to be lulled into thinking that carefully paced changes are somehow less threatening to their careers.

Companies that string out the integration process invariably come under harsh criticism from people at all levels of the organization. Given their preference, employees would vote in favor of expediting the process—for example, integrate, consolidate, terminate, reorganize, or redirect as necessary. They just want to get on with it, so they can get on with their careers and make their personal adjustments to whatever happens to them as individuals.

Sometimes acquirers are slow in announcing major changes that are forthcoming because they fear personnel will make pre-emptive moves that will damage company operations. For example, top management may withhold information about a plant shutdown or a major layoff, thinking people will bail out ahead of time.

This is another situation, though, where a counterintuitive move is likely to get the best results. If management waits until the last minute to spring the bad news, everybody gets jolted once again. The trust level takes another hit. People are likely to resent the company's approach to the situation and to feel even more need to protect their own careers.

The counterintuitive approach would be for management to be very up-front with employees who are to be affected, giving them as much advance notice as possible and offering them equitable severance arrangements. The company should explain the important role they can play in the phasedown, plus make it clear how much their help and support are needed. Then top management should ask them straightforwardly to commit to staying until the wrap-up date.

When the company takes this tack and provides strong and sincere psychological reinforcement to the people who sign on for the closeout period, there is virtually never a problem of people jumping ship and wrecking the phasedown. They usually stay until the very last day, and then leave on good terms, respecting the company for the way it handled the situation.

This honorable, trustworthy way of handling such a difficult situation is not lost on the people who remain either. As incumbents who stay with the firm, their respect for the company grows. The trust level is protected and even upgraded. It's the sort of thing that can cast a very long (and favorable) shadow.

Another very strong argument for moving rapidly in making merger-related changes relates to the "time window" for change.

It works like this. Being acquired or merged has a profound impact on the target company. It destabilizes the organization. Things get knocked around in this time of upheaval. The organization is in a state of flux—up in the air—and there is a brief opportunity to reshape many aspects of the company before things settle back down and crystallize into the same old routines.

But the window of opportunity is open only for a brief and unspecific period of time. People are expecting change, and the circumstances are right. Top management should seize the opportunity before the window closes. The same changes, sought at a later date, after the time window has shut and the organizational dissonance has faded, can meet with extreme resistance.

COACHING POINTS

1. Move fast. To the extent possible, changes should be made in an informed and purposeful fashion, but ordinarily a little precision can be sacrificed for speed.

2. Make sure the first few actions made vis-á-vis the acquired firm telegraph the right kind of messages.

3. If management does elect to proceed slowly, at least take

active steps to get to know as much as possible about the acquisition (for example, conduct surveys, do management evaluations, etc.).

4. Be alert to the "window of opportunity" the merger provides for making needed changes. The changes that are made rapidly are usually made more easily.

5. Be willing to risk making some mistakes. Moving too slowly invariably leads to mistakes, too, although they frequently are not readily apparent. As General Patton maintained, "A good plan acted on today can be better than a perfect plan acted on later."

6. While striving to move rapidly, keep in mind that merger integration activities often take longer than you expect. Be careful of announcing unrealistic "hero dates" that you prove unable to meet. That often results in more "violations of expectations."

FIXING THINGS THAT AIN'T BROKEN

This mistake is usually caused by the parent company. It is a common failing of staff people in the acquiring firm who descend on the acquisition, the so-called corporate sea gulls, who:

> Fly in on the company plane, squawk a lot, eat your food, crap all over you, and then fly home.

Sometimes it's not so much *what* is done, as *how* it's done:

- Without adequate explanation.
- Without negotiating the changes.
- With a superior "we-acquired-you" attitude.
- Without an understanding or respect for the ramifications.

"Fixing" or changing something, in and of itself, might be fine— but it may upset a delicate balance somewhere that is critically valuable.

What usually gets fixed in the acquisition? Things like financial systems, compensation plans, procedures, and reporting practices. So often parent company management changes things like these to conform with the way they are handled in the parent firm, without ever really questioning or challenging the decision to make the shift.

Fixing things unnecessarily can cost a lot of money, dollars that might be spent on better efforts. Fixing things that aren't broken also consumes time and effort. It adds to the job stress because, first, it takes some work time to make the changes and, second, people often have to struggle learning how to do things the new way. Often the company's resources (time, people, money) need to be invested elsewhere, where the payoff is far better.

Naturally, fixing things means making changes, and changes mean more adjustments for employees, probably one of the last things they need in the postmerger environment. Usually the transition period after the merger is complicated enough without any unneeded changes being dumped on people. Why add to the stress and confusion?

Finally, managers need to guard against fixing or changing things in the acquisition without also providing sufficient coaching or training for people on how to do things the new way.

An important point here is that acquired company personnel often are afraid to ask for help, or are embarrassed to admit they can't do things the new way. Instead of straightforwardly confessing their problems and inabilities, they are much more likely to gripe, sullenly resist the changes, or just give up and perhaps quit.

COACHING POINTS

1. When things that aren't broken are going to be fixed, explain to people the rationale for making the change. Try to make it make sense to them.

2. Approach the changes in such a way that acquired company personnel feel some sense of ownership of the changes.

3. Be sure people get the coaching and training they need to do things the new way.

4. Stop, at the outset, to consider whether it really should be "fixed."

5. If management is intent on fixing something, why not fix something that really is broken? Do that for people in the acquired company, and the parent firm has a chance of being a hero.

UNDERCOMMUNICATING AND LOSING TOUCH

With mergers being a time of transition and "growing pains," the normal communication channels don't work as well as usual. Information may not flow fast enough, or to the right people. Sometimes key information doesn't flow at all, as employees are uneasy about speaking out.

The result? Problems can go unattended. Questions sometimes don't get answered. People's concerns and worries may not be fully understood by higher management. Finally, good ideas can get lost in the shuffle. The usual information networks get balled up. They simply won't carry the freight.

There are 10 main reasons why companies that are being acquired and merged require extra communication efforts:

1. The rumor mill causes a lot of information warp. There are many unreliable messages floating around that need to be identified and cleared up.

2. The "truth" keeps changing, and is often dead on arrival. Decisions are made, announced, then promptly changed. People can't keep up with what's happening.

3. Merging companies commonly have different ways of communicating—different styles, different vocabularies. This often leads to confusion and misunderstanding.

4. Information often has to travel further, following new and different routes. That takes time—sometimes more time than management can afford.

5. It may be unclear exactly who needs to be included in the information loop. It's easy for messages to get lost or miss key people.

6. Some people are afraid to communicate openly and honestly. Important messages may never be sent, or they may be so watered down they are not taken seriously by others.

7. People are more skeptical and mistrusting in the merger environment. It takes more of a communication effort to convince them.

8. People are troubled by the ambiguity and uncertainty. They desire more information and better answers than usual.

9. Managers become more wary and guarded—less willing to commit themselves, make decisions, or communicate freely for fear of ending up with egg on their faces.
10. More things of significance are happening. There simply is more news, more change, more to be communicated.

When merger difficulties do develop, 75 percent of them have their roots in communication problems. In fact, at the very time company communication needs to be better than ever, it's often at its worst.

And the trouble is that communication problems never seem to remain *just* communication problems. They end up causing productivity problems, morale problems, and—eventually—profitability problems. Work becomes more frustrating and stressful for everyone. As for the job of managing, well, it's impossible for the people in charge to run things right if they're not adequately informed.

John Teets, chairman and CEO of Greyhound Corporation, made this statement when urging senior managers in a new acquisition to keep the information pipelines open:

> It's extremely difficult for people at the top to stay in touch with what's going on lower down in the company. When I'm going to be at a meeting, the other executives and managers tell their people, "If Teets doesn't ask, don't tell him anything. If he asks, say it like this." I'm the guy who gets on the elevator and conversation dies. I sit at the end of the cesspool. By the time it gets to me it's pure enough to drink.

The organizational confusion brought on by mergers creates many opportunities for information flow to get short-circuited or bottlenecked. Sometimes people are afraid to be bearers of bad news. And again, managers are chronically unwilling to be open and honest in asking for help or to admit they're having problems, particularly if the merger situation has resulted in their working for a new boss.

In all fairness, it should also be pointed out that in the merging process managers sometimes just get overloaded with work and feel they are unable to take on any additional problems. As one executive put it, "We got to where we didn't want to lift the rock and see what was under it."

When it reaches the point that managers are this overburdened, they become guilty of avoiding, denying, and downplaying problems. They lose touch.

Granted, there are some merger problems that will take care of themselves as time goes by. But there will be others that simply grow worse and create additional problems that place still more demands on managerial time.

Because communication is a two-way street, managers and executives have to work at keeping in touch with their people through downward communication as well. During the merger integration period it's common to find managers who isolate themselves in their offices and actually hold fewer meetings than usual. They may become more guarded and evasive too.

Savvy managers are the ones who visit the front lines and get down in the trenches. They go out and gather their own data. This enables them to get more current information and different perspectives. In the process, they will also likely boost morale and enjoy more success as leaders.

Sometimes parent company managers don't communicate very much with people in an acquisition out of their conviction that it would be best to take a hands-off stance. But people in the acquisition usually want all the information they can get. Actually, they suffer from what might be described as "approach-avoidance conflict." They don't want the parent company to interfere, but neither do they want to be ignored.

It does take a careful communication effort on the part of parent company officials. Acquired personnel are inclined to overreact because they don't have a good feel for how the new parent company communicates.

Acquirees may take a casual, offhand remark, or a general suggestion, and read it as a directive. Then they may exaggerate still further in instructing their own subordinates to implement the idea. So what may have been just a thought becomes a dictate, with people feeling they have had no chance to counter with alternative suggestions or reasons why the idea wasn't appropriate.

The basic point is this key managers in the parent company have little opportunity to make *insignificant* remarks. Practically everything they say is taken seriously, studied for innuendo, or held up to the light for subtle implications.

Parent company personnel must constantly watch what they say and always check for understanding.

COACHING POINTS

1. Establish merger-integration teams at various levels, comprised of people from both organizations who can represent the different functions in the organization.

2. Provide regular written communication to employees that contains merger update information. This can be a specially created flyer, a regular newsletter, or other house organs that go to all people.

3. Develop and distribute periodic videotapes of senior executives discussing merger-related matters. These can be delivered as "fireside chats" or more formal presentations.

4. Provide employees a toll-free telephone number they can use anonymously to report problems, ask questions, clear up rumors, or make suggestions vis-a-vis the merger. It is best to contract with an external provider for this kind of service. That helps protect confidentiality by letting respondents call in with total anonymity.

5. Practice MBWA (management by walking around). Circulate. Visit with people. Ask questions. Shoot the bull. Go see people, and be seen, as that communicates something important too.

6. Conduct periodic barnstorming tours of plants, divisions, satellite facilities, and field offices. Some should be scheduled, perhaps some done in an impromptu fashion.

7. There should be more meetings, not less.

8. After three or four months—six months at the most—conduct a merger survey to see how things are tracking. Use an outside consulting firm that understands merger dynamics and can help you conduct this study with a very specialized survey instrument that will identify the most likely problem spots. After 12 to 18 months, conduct a more conventional employee attitude and opinion survey in the merged organization (or in the acquisition, if it is being left more or less as a stand-alone unit.)

9. Do whatever works. Keep in touch through means that are

either formal or informal. Some communication efforts should be carefully scheduled, others implemented when the opportunity presents itself.

CHAPTER FOUR

Managing Employees through the Three Merger Stages

As mergers bring changes, so those changes create a sense of loss for employees. The natural response of the human being is to mourn those losses.

The resulting pattern of feelings and emotions is very consistent from one merger to the next. Some corporate marriages are more gut-wrenching and traumatic than others, of course, but virtually always there is a period of grief and mourning that ensues.

What creates the pervasive sense of loss? Why is there such a predictable emotional response from all layers of the corporate hierarchy, from the captain of the ship down to the people who are chained to the oars deep in the organization?

The first loss is generic—it's the loss of a sense of security. Because mergers provoke so much uncertainty and ambiguity, and because the trust level ordinarily goes into a tailspin, many people feel their career stability has suddenly been stripped away.

Then more tangible issues come into play: Employees lose their boss, co-workers, or perhaps their own jobs. Highly valued feelings of camaraderie may vanish, along with one's power base, perks, and privileges. The intangible but all-important feelings of belonging, as well as the sense of pride in the company and its culture, are frequently sacrificed.

Naturally, many people are going to feel that the merger/acquisition event has come at great personal cost to them as individuals. Ordinarily they are not expecting it to be such a psychological jolt, either, and even that element of surprise adds to the personal stress they experience.

There are three very predictable stages in the grieving process (see Figure 3):

Stage 1: Shock and numbness
Stage 2: Suffering
Stage 3: Resolution

In the process of being acquired and merged, some employees will be affected more profoundly than others. Also some people just possess more emotional resilience than others and thus are not affected as severely or for as long. It's quite possible, too, that some people get lucky, gaining much and feeling no particular personal loss as a result of their firm's merger.

Those who do experience significant personal loss, though, will proceed through this normal emotional cycle.

Each of the three stages serves necessary functions. And movement from one stage to the next is contingent upon the successful completion of the preceding phase. It seems that one has to move through this healing process in a sequential fashion, and that there are no shortcuts.

Management can deal with people's feelings and behaviors in each stage in such a way as to either facilitate the healing process or complicate things and prolong the psychological pain. The key comes in knowing what to expect from people and what that implies by way of a needed managerial response.

FIGURE 3: The Three Merger Stages

	Stage 1	*Stage 2*	*Stage 3*
Employee reactions	Shock and numbness	Suffering	Resolution
Appropriate managerial responses	Manage the trauma	Provide intensive care	Oversee rehabilitation

---

STAGE 1: SHOCK AND NUMBNESS

Typically this stage begins when people first get hit with the news that their organization is being acquired and merged.

Sometimes the shock doesn't occur until things develop on a

much more personal level, such as an employee finding out that he or she works in a division that will be shut down. So often though, an entire work force is stunned by an unexpected announcement stating that their firm is being acquired or merged.

The key characteristic of this first emotional stage is, paradoxically, the absence of emotions. People react numbly. It is as if they have been anesthetized emotionally. At the outset there is not much of a feeling of pain or psychological distress. Rather, people seem to have difficulty assessing the full significance of what they hear. Frequently there are expressions of disbelief such as "That can't be!" or, "You're kidding!"

Sometimes there are panic reactions, and it also is fairly common to see flashes of anger. The really strong displays of feelings however, are reserved for Stage 2.

Employee behaviors in Stage 1 reflect the fact that people are in a daze. They may seem to be almost immobilized. They are not mentally very well suited to do more than carry out their basic job functions, and even then it may seem like they are in trance. They go through the motions, but it is as if they are on automatic pilot.

In Stage 1, people seem to be preoccupied with what is happening to them, yet at the same time it appears they have difficulty grasping the full impact of the merger. They are still mentally digesting the news.

As a result, managers find it hard to get people's full attention. Employees' concentration skills suffer and they don't always hear accurately enough. They can easily miss all or part of a message aimed in their direction. Performance also suffers because they are more disorganized, less productive, and inclined to let time frames slip.

For most people Stage 1 is rather brief—the shock soon wears off, and the pain sets in. Still, Stage 1 feelings and behaviors call for management attention.

Management Do's and Don'ts. The following guidelines can be helpful when dealing with people who are struggling with the dynamics of this first stage in the grieving process:

1. Get everything out in the open. Communicate as complete a set of facts as possible about the merger story.

2. Be realistic and speak the truth, preparing people for what's to come in terms of actual merger issues as well as grief issues, rather than promising "blue sky."

3. Don't be deceived or misled by people's initial calm and lack of emotion. The worst is yet to come.

4. Offer instructions and directions more slowly and carefully. In fact, it is advisable to put more of this in writing than one would under ordinary circumstances.

5. Check for understanding. When people are in shock, so to speak, they tend not to process data very well in their heads. It's important to start working immediately on rumor prevention.

6. Outline specific assignments for others rather than leaving things vague and ambiguous. Be more generous in providing subordinates job structure and guidance.

7. Assign definite timetables regarding when work is to be completed. Organizational slippage starts early in the merger integration process.

8. Be patient. Take more time with people. Be more long-suffering and tolerant of employees' idiosyncrasies that are the result of Stage 1 stress.

9. Be nondefensive. Guard against fighting back when some of the reckless anger happens to be thrown in your direction.

10. Check more closely for errors. It's easy for people to make mistakes or let things slip through the cracks when they are in the Stage 1 frame of mind.

11. Show better follow-up in general. Monitor closely. Brush fires are a common problem in merging companies because people aren't paying sufficient attention to what they're doing. Management has to check up on things more regularly.

12. Establish shorter time frames for goals and objectives. In Stage 1, people are highly distractible. They need more of a near-term focus.

STAGE 2: SUFFERING

If Stage 1 can be considered the trauma event, Stage 2 is when the victim begins to feel the hurt.

Now the feelings become more pronounced and more visible. The shock wears off and the reality of the merger registers. Pain sets in.

In Stage 2, fear and a sense of insecurity replace the surprise and disbelief of the initial phase. Managers have to deal with a surge of emotions that covers a broad spectrum of feelings—for example, anxiety regarding the future, distrust, self-pity, frustration, bitterness, depression, and even guilt.

Now employee behavior becomes much more unpredictable because it is founded more on emotion and less on logic or objective thinking. The job of running the company becomes much more complicated for management, partially because of the emotional state of subordinates and also because managers and executives themselves are often going through the very same emotional turmoil. They personally are experiencing the same feelings and behaviors they are scrambling to manage in others.

Work usually becomes quite disorganized and confusing in Stage 2.

Employees jockey for position, test new leaders, mourn the loss of old leaders, and romanticize the past. Endless hours are wasted while employees worry and brood, trade rumors, and keep going over and over the same issues.

One of the common stress reactions is to resist change, as people cling to familiar, traditional approaches and strive to protect the status quo. The play-it-safe stance that prevails makes people want to stick with habitual behavior patterns rather than to experiment or take risks. The uncertainty and reluctance to make decisions also adds to the growing corporate inertia.

The hostility that is so characteristic of Stage 2 is handled differently by people. Some act out their anger, resentment, and frustration in an impulsive, temperamental fashion. Others bottle up their feelings inside, but may become unresponsive and withdrawn. Apathy, loss of confidence, plus feelings of powerlessness and helplessness, prompt some people to more or less give up. Loss of commitment is one of the most damaging developments seen in Stage 2.

In this stage of the merger integration process there is much to be done. Companies are in a hurry. But getting through Stage 2 successfully takes time, patience, and understanding.

Management has to allow the healing process to be played out—hurts can be doctored and pain can be attended, but wounds still take time to heal.

The mergers that go bad—the ones that get logged in the failure statistics—are the ones that never really manage to pull out of Stage 2. They never get out of "intensive care."

Management Do's and Don'ts. Managing a work force that is bogged down in Stage 2 is a treacherous exercise. Employees are inclined to resist help, or be blameful of the boss, and behave in self-destructive ways. It takes real insight and skill, plus managerial maturity, to handle the situation.

1. Don't be frightened or annoyed by the emotional display. It's natural, and understandable, in the scheme of things.
2. Provide opportunities for people to ventilate. Instead of disallowing employees' feelings—instead of arguing, getting upset, or discounting their problems—let the feelings spew forth. People need to ventilate their feelings and work through them. Let them lick their wounds.
3. Listen to people. Hear them out. That's the only way to discern the insurgents from those people who are simply suffering and who are being overwhelmed by their emotions. It's important to distinguish true troublemakers from the folks who are simply having trouble managing their feelings.
4. Be supportive, nurturing, and affirming. A little understanding and "TLC" go a long way in Stage 2. Someone has said, "Children need love, especially when they don't deserve it." The same can be said about employees.
5. Try to provide success experiences for people. They need encouragement and any other confidence-builders that are available.
6. Motivate to the maximum extent. In Stage 2 there typically is a severe dropoff in self-motivation, which means management has to take up the slack and provide additional inspiration.
7. Continue, as in Stage 1, to offer more in terms of hands-on management. Give people more specific marching orders, more guidance and direction, than usual.
8. Keep people involved. The tendency is for job commitment to weaken, and more participation can help counter this. If they are charged with merger integration responsibilities, they feel less impotent and less like victims.
9. Be tolerant of mistakes and intolerant of inertia. Urge decisiveness and an action orientation.

10. Require more of employees. Now is the time to "raise the bar," and place greater work challenges before them. (Otherwise, though, seek to reduce sources of stress in the work environment.)

11. Re-recruit key incumbents—all of them that the company wants to keep. Do this with the same intensity that would be invested in recruiting an outsider to join the organization.

12. Put more into communication efforts. That would include meetings, memos, written instructions, casual conversation, and just circulating among the work force.

13. Don't hide bad news (but don't let it drive good news away). Minimize surprises.

14. Maintain more of a managerial presence, or a higher profile in the work group. Visibility is needed. Be there.

15. Spend more time with people one-on-one.

16. Expect people to be disorganized, "spaced out," and inefficient. But be careful not to reinforce helplessness.

Stage 2 is the high-risk phase of the merger integration process so far as people's feelings and behaviors are concerned. When this period is prolonged by poor management practices, organizations significantly increase the odds that they will join the statistics on merger failures. The paradox, though, is that in moving through the stressful events and disturbing problems of Stage 2, the company actually is on the road that leads to recovery. This is the "valley of the shadows" that has to be crossed en route to Stage 3.

STAGE 3: RESOLUTION

Clear signs of recovery connote the beginning of Stage 3. If Stage 2 was the merger coma that required managerial intensive care, Stage 3 is the rehabilitation ward.

Now people begin to feel better and the organization, as a whole, is getting well. People begin adjusting to the situation and personally come to grips with what the merger has wrought in their individual lives and careers.

The negative emotions so characteristic of the troubled times in Stage 2 taper off in this phase. With resolution comes a more balanced perspective on the part of people. They weigh the pros and cons of the situation in a more fair-minded, dispassionate, realistic fashion.

People still may worry about possible future changes, and dislike various aspects of the merger setup, but finally there is acceptance of the situation. Or, perhaps more accurately for a number of people, there is resignation, as they come to the realization that things are going to be the way they are and that to fight is futile.

The negativism of the suffering period gives way to curiosity in Stage 3, just as the pessimism is replaced by a hint of hopefulness. If nurtured by management, this can quickly develop into optimism and possibly even true enthusiasm for the future.

Periodically, people may experience emotional setbacks from the aftershocks of continuing merger developments. Ordinarily, though, there seems to be a new level of psychological resilience (derived from earlier Stage 2 struggles) that serves people well and enables them to bounce back more quickly.

Stage 3 behavior is less self-oriented, reflecting people's growing sense of security. They are less involved in protecting themselves and avoiding mistakes, while more focused on getting the job done and making progress with business. They are more action-oriented and purposeful, more decisive. There are fewer hidden agendas and not as much political game-playing.

It is important to remember, though, that the organization is still in the recovery phase. It has not fully regained its strength. There is still a substantial amount of vulnerability that management must respect.

Management Do's and Don'ts. Managers and executives continue in Stage 3 to play a critical role in managing the transition and change that the merger has generated. These key guidelines help ensure proper closure in the grief and mourning process:

1. Don't rush the grieving process. Let Stage 3 play itself out.
2. Expect setbacks, at least with some people.
3. Respect the fact that some people grieve longer than others, whether they "lost" more or just suffer differently.
4. Don't assume others are where you are emotionally.

5. When hopefulness and curiosity begin to surface, reinforce that attitude change. Fan the flame of hope.

6. Continue team-building efforts. In Stage 3, people better equipped psychologically begin building or rebuilding relationships. Significant strides in team play can be accomplished now.

7. Since there is less need in general to attend to people's psychological needs, do so selectively. Identify those persons who are lagging behind in the grieving process, and seek to bring them along more rapidly.

8. Continue to manage closely. Even in Stage 3 there is likely to be an excessive amount of ambiguity and uncertainty that can easily interfere with performance.

9. Don't get complacent or lazy. Again, the drill is not over yet. Guard against relapses.

Senior executives, in particular, seem to have a temptation to want to dictate closure to this merger recovery process. After a few months, a company president will declare, "The merger is over. Now I expect you to get on with business."

The point is, such a statement, made either as a request or order, can hardly accomplish anything positive. Usually the people further down in the company expect more changes, more aftershocks. And they often have not yet come to grips with preceding changes. They are not "over it." And a proclamation by top management doesn't change that fact.

Yogi Berra captures the truth of the situation in his classic remark, "It's not over til it's over."

A FOUR-STEP PROCESS FOR DEALING WITH LOSS

Management that is insensitive to employees and their sense of loss will encounter troublesome resistance during merger transition periods.

A person's work, a career, is too central to one's sense of self and basic identity to be treated so casually (or disregarded altogether) as it often is when firms are being acquired and merged. Helping people through the period of loss, the time of grief and mourning, has a significant payoff. Conversely, ignoring the situation and expecting things to take care of themselves gets to be unbelievably pricey.

A game plan for managing merger change consists of four distinct steps:

1. Presenting a historical summary that vividly captures the essence of that which will be lost or terminated.
2. Giving a good rationale for the changes.
3. Honoring the past.
4. Showing linkages between the past and the future.

The first step in this process is aimed toward giving employees a sense of closure. The past is scanned, important aspects of history are identified, and then these are woven into a composite summary.

For example, a manufacturer of eye care products acquired a competing firm and proceeded to merge the acquisition (which was actually larger) into the parent organization. The history of the target company was a rather dramatic tale, complete with heroes, fascinating war stories, significant accomplishments and problems, and high aspirations. All of these issues, and many others, were blended into a comprehensive, very credible summary of the firm's past.

Such a "history book" doesn't have to be totally true, but it must be believable. The summary has to get across the essence of what is being lost, and present that story as a *prelude.*

The next step amounts to giving people good reasons for the forthcoming changes. Here the argument is introduced to justify the losses. The rationale should include justification for the kind of change that is being initiated, the scope of the change, plus the reasons for making the changes at this particular point in time.

Next comes the ritual of honoring the past. This is basically like a ceremonial eulogy that both acknowledges and celebrates that which is being left behind. This represents another major step toward closure, much as a funeral does when people experience the loss of a loved one.

The fourth and final step in the process is to demonstrate the continuity between the past (what is being lost) and the future. People need to feel that at least some of the things they valued about what is being lost will somehow be preserved, that these things will survive in the postmerger scheme of things. This idea of continuity is a subtle but critically important matter, as it supports the belief that past values will live on.

This sketch of the four tasks that need to be performed in managing merger changes can be a helpful framework in preparing speeches, company announcements, or written materials.

COACHING POINTS

1. Get prepared to manage a period of "corporate convalescence." The manager's job during the merger integration process becomes as much a matter of conducting organizational therapy as supervising.

2. Mergers lead to hundreds of distractions. Employees need "focusing" by management. There is a need for much more effort in giving subordinates structure and direction.

3. Work aggressively to provide people a sense of closure. Move through the fog of ambiguity. Resolve things like chain of command, reporting relationships, procedures, or the transfer/termination/"what is my job?" set of issues.

Managing Resistance to Change

There are two basic assumptions managers can safely make about organizations that are being acquired and merged:

1. There will be changes.
2. There will be resistance to change.

Organizations are never totally static. They evolve, adjust, and react to many different forces in the environment. They evoke change themselves.

Even if the parent company takes a hands-off stance, even if it wishes to let the target company remain a stand-alone acquisition, the employees still experience it as psychological change. Furthermore, routine changes that might have happened anyway commonly get blamed on the merger. It makes a good whipping boy.

Ordinarily, though, it is easy to identify a number of fairly significant changes that come from being acquired and merged. People often have to adjust to a new boss, a switch in management philosophy, different procedures, or a shift in the organization's emphasis. There are employees who get relocated, reorganized, and released. Workers have to adapt to a different corporate culture and pursue new goals and objectives.

Usually the change is undermanaged.

Executives and managers regularly underestimate just how complicated and stressful the change process is for everyone. As a result, there is a lot more wreckage—both personal and organizational—than there should be.

Too often companies have great weddings that turn into bad

marriages because the people in charge do not handle transition and change very well. And usually it is the people side of a merger that is undermanaged more than the technical side of things.

WHERE RESISTANCE COMES FROM

The potential for resistance to change increases in the merger/acquisition setting because people grow concerned and fearful. They become much more alert to distressing events. The self-preservation mentality makes them hypersensitive to change. They get jumpy and uneasy about what may happen and how they personally might be affected.

The trust level is sagging, too, and their heightened skepticism makes them feel more vulnerable to negative effects of change.

Ironically, employees do expect change, and even want it in certain respects. Logic tells them there are bound to be changes due to the merger, and they want to find out what they are.

They hate suspense. Waiting and wondering seems to be even more painful than knowing awful truths. Still, when the changes are announced, and even more so when they are implemented, people naturally resist.

Initial resistance often develops simply because people do not have a good understanding of the rationale for the changes. Frequently employees are told what will happen, or how things will change, but they are not given any explanation. Top management does not share the logic or reasoning behind the action.

In fact, sometimes people resist a merger in general because they are kept in the dark and can only speculate what the forthcoming changes may be. Or word of an impending change can be pumped out by the rumor mill without any background data regarding justification for the change.

Under these circumstances, people may be against change merely because they misperceive exactly what is happening or why it is happening. A warped or flawed view of the situation may be the main problem.

In the absence of good information flow, where people don't have enough facts to work with, they get mixed up and more wary. That wariness or caution easily translates into resistance. This is particularly true when employees don't really understand where the changes might be taking them.

As much as anything, they may be fighting the ambiguity and blur regarding what the end result of the changes will be. A big percentage of people have a low tolerance for ambiguity, preferring a stabilized, predictable world.

But mergers destabilize things and create a high level of "organizational dissonance." The natural striving for equilibrium or homeostasis explains some of the resistance.

The more employees understand what the alternatives are and the trade-offs that are involved, the better they can buy into the situation and accept change. But even if they have good insight into the situation, they may be resistant for fear of their own inability to measure up to the new way of doing things. If they feel inadequate, or question their ability to cope with the change from a skills standpoint, it's natural for them to decry the changes.

None of us really likes to fail. For that matter, we usually don't even like having to give up an approach or methodology where we are comfortably effective (perhaps even expert) to adopt a different set of practices or tactics we handle less adroitly and maybe even awkwardly. When merger-related changes require people to do things in new and different ways, that added vulnerability to failure is simply unattractive to people.

In the process of growing up—as children, adolescents, and even adults—people come to expect praise and other rewards as their performance improves. When performance deteriorates, positive reinforcement from others becomes more scarce, and even self-satisfaction diminishes.

So it's not hard to understand why people bow up and resist change or new approaches where they are likely to be seen as less proficient. Sure, most people like growth and self-development—but what they like is the end result, and not the price tag. Very often the cost of growth is resented.

Another factor that complicates this issue of taking chances and risking failure is that people sometimes don't know how they'll be graded. Having a new boss, for example, is like playing the game with a new scorekeeper. Acquiring companies often have different standards that aren't communicated very well to the newcomers.

This situation, at least indirectly, increases the odds for performance shortfall or outright failure. That's not a very attractive setup, and it helps explain why acquired company personnel lack enthusiasm for certain changes.

People need to be able to see some kind of favorable payoff for doing things the new way, or for buying into changes. If they are not informed about what's in it for them, there really is no good motivation to fuel the new behaviors. The management challenge is to provide an incentive that is potent enough to make employees want the changes to work.

All too often the changes mean more work, that the job is going to get harder, or that employees will stand to lose in one way or another (i.e., status, freedom, meaningful relationships, power, privileges, etc.). Since most people don't particularly enjoy personal sacrifice, they will resist having something taken away unless *something* of value is offered in return.

Resistance to change is one way employees have of fighting back. It can be their way of "getting even."

They may not be able to prevent certain changes or undesirable events, but sometimes they figure out how to resist some other things that higher management wants. Thus, their resistance to change may be an issue of displacement, where they take their feelings out on the best target that is available to them. This is a particular problem because it means that sometimes top management ends up fighting symptoms instead of true causes.

There are, of course, plenty of situations where change is vigorously resisted because of people's earnest belief that the change is wrong, a bad plan, or flat out won't work. This conviction can be well founded, based on employees' experience or insights into the situation.

Management needs to keep in mind the fact that resistance can be very well intentioned, even noble and courageous. Self-interest is not always at work. Resistance to change is not always solid evidence that people are being oppositional, negativistic malcontents.

As a matter of fact, most people who can be observed resisting merger-related changes firmly believe that their stance is justified and, quite often, in the best interest of the organization. They do not see themselves as troublemakers. If accused of being obstructionists and given subtle or clear-cut threats, they typically just become more demoralized and entrenched in their resistance.

This is particularly true anytime the proposed changes are

inconsistent with the person's self-image or personal values. Resistance is virtually guaranteed anytime an employee is expected to perform in a fashion that is in conflict with "the sort of person I am."

The self-concept or self-image has a remarkably powerful influence over an individual's behavior, just as corporate culture governs the collective behavior of people in an organization.

When an acquirer's expectations and proposed changes are out of phase with one's self-image or the acquisition's corporate culture, there are going to be problems. Resistance is almost a given. Moreover, the resister invariably sees his or her behavior as a virtue and views the parent company's push for change as an offense.

Noncompliance, then, is a tricky thing for managers and executives to handle. It is essential to know where the resistance is grounded.

It is quite possible that resistance to change simply results from emotional overload. Merger-related changes can be overwhelming, at least for some people. The pressure may be too much.

Under high stress and trauma people tend to regress. They cling to the familiar, the tried-and-true. It's an instinctive move to conserve one's psychological resources by taking fewer risks and incurring less demands. This sort of resistance to change is a very natural coping move. It's a search for safety on the part of the employee, not a deliberate effort to be contrary or rebellious.

It's important to realize that sometimes people resist change for reasons they personally (a) cannot articulate, (b) don't really understand, or (c) won't level about with you. As a result, a lot of the resistance to change is never really understood by the people in charge. It gets misinterpreted and is attacked with the wrong weapons.

HOW PEOPLE RESIST

The myriad ways in which people resist change are as much a reflection of individual personalities as of the merger circumstances that are involved. Given identical situations, two people of different temperaments would in all probability react differently. One employee may fiercely resist a change, while a co-worker who stands to be affected in much the same way accepts the change and goes on.

Many factors come into play: mental attitude, emotional resilience, ambition, stress tolerance, previous experience, age, self-confidence, the individual's perspective—the list could go on and on.

A common trap managers and executives get caught in comes from attributing one's own perceptions, values, feelings, and needs to other people. In other words, we often assume people are made like ourselves. When it comes to managing resistance to change, that can be a treacherous assumption. Many of the people involved in a merger situation simply don't look at things the same way as the people they work with or for.

To simplify the issue of how people resist change, it might help to identify the two main behavioral styles: active resistance and passive resistance. Everyone who opposes change will exhibit a little of both, but at the same time each person will have his or her own primary stance that is most characteristic.

Active resistance is overt. It's visible. You can see it with the naked eye. In fact, active resistance is usually purposeful rather than accidental. In other words, employees who are active resisters are deliberate in letting their opposition show.

It's important, however, to differentiate between active resistance that is counterproductive and that which is more appropriately labeled "constructive conflict."

The first behavior is a sort of negativism that gets in the way of the merger. The second behavior is healthy and serves a purpose. Whereas active resistance is frequently self-oriented, constructive conflict is not. Active resistance may be borne out of "personal pain," but constructive conflict practically always is a sign that a person has guts.

Top management may want to rid the company of troublesome resistance to change. The danger is that it will be done at the expense of healthy disagreement.

To complicate things still further, there is the problem of passive resistance. This is covert opposition, or resistance that is masked. The odds are it is much more pernicious and ultimately more dangerous to the success of the merger than active resistance. Passive resisters are the invisible threat. They offer proof that, at least in the merger/acquisition arena, what you don't see, hear, or know can hurt you.

One form of passive resistance is characterized by devious behavior—the quiet insurgents. Top management recruits for this group when it develops the reputation for shooting messengers who carry bad news. This covert opposition frequently develops because the company has driven resistance underground, creating a corps of silent saboteurs.

In the other category of passive resisters are the people suffering from "decommitment." They are not so much an obstacle to the merger as they are a drag on its progress. The curse of these covert resisters is corporate inertia. The people who comprise this group often are frustrated and burned out, to the point that they have sort of given up. Some get so fed up with the stress and aggravations of the merger process that they quit and leave. Others quit and stay.

The point is that resistance takes many forms and has many faces. Surface appearances can be deceiving. Outspoken critics may be the merger's best friend, while those employees who display mute acceptance of change may seriously interfere with the integration process.

STEPS TOWARD OVERCOMING RESISTANCE TO CHANGE

Many merger/acquisition events are likely to be unpopular, at least with those groups of employees who are negatively affected. What people don't like, they will probably resist.

Management cannot keep everyone happy. But a number of things can be done to overcome some of the resistance and minimize that which remains.

1. *Explain the reasons for the change.* Usually the best steps in dealing with problems are the preventive ones.

Perhaps the most effective way to minimize resistance is to make sure people in the organization have a good understanding of the rationale for the changes.

The people in charge should be very open, very willing to share their perspectives or the line of reasoning that led to the changes. When this sort of information is communicated, the odds increase that everyone else will come to see the move as appropriate.

But even those personnel who disagree with the logic behind the change, and who are personally against it, are far more likely to accept the situation than if they had it shoved at them without any explanation.

So giving people in the work force the story behind merger changes is helpful in several ways. First, some people will be persuaded that the move was an appropriate one. Others will not be convinced, but at least they will understand why it's happening, and therefore will accept it. Finally, still others who neither agree with nor understand the reasoning behind the change will elect not to fight it, because at least someone took the pains to try and explain the situation for them.

There are several guidelines to follow in getting the message across:

A.   Prepare well. Instead of winging it or shooting from the hip in making the announcement, do some good homework. The explanation should be well organized, easy to understand, and believable.

B.   Allow sufficient time to get the message across effectively. This may call for more than one meeting. Things of importance typically need to be communicated several times, and in different ways.

C.   Point out specifically what will change, how the change will unfold, and, to the extent possible, the expected time frame.

D.   Sell the changes. Point out the advantages or positive aspects of the changes to the people who are affected.

E.   Point out the probabilities of success in implementing the changes.

F.   Identify your support systems for the changes.

G.   Explain what you need from the employees, and specifically ask for it.

H.   Acknowledge the potential problems. Say what's real, instead of only hyping or "promoting" the change. Get people prepared psychologically for both the pros and cons of the change.

2. *Level with people about the pathway to change.* There is a need for people to understand what the road to change looks like—that typically the pathway is a sequence of events where

things get worse before they get better.

Several brief examples may help make this point. First, think of the young boy who wants to learn how to ride a bicycle. He can walk without any problem and generally gets where he wants to go. But his mobility actually becomes less successful when he starts trying to ride the bike. He falls down, bruises an arm, scrapes a knee, and cannot make forward progress as well as if he were walking. His mobility actually deteriorates. But he keeps working at the change, and pretty soon is traveling in a faster, more pleasurable style than he was when merely walking.

Similarly, consider the example of a woman with circulatory problems who enters the hospital to have heart surgery. She may very well walk into the hospital feeling quite fine. However, they will wheel her out of the operating room flat on her back, keep her in intensive care for a while, and generally weaken her physical condition such that she cannot be very active for a period of days. So in a sense she's gotten worse, but that's part of the pathway toward overall improved physical health.

Mergers, and the changes they bring, typically reflect the same sort of sequence. Top management needs to prepare employees for this scenario.

Growth (and mergers usually imply organizational growth) generally carries a little bit of pain and discomfort with it, and these growing pains are part of the process that people need to understand and expect.

Pete Silas, chairman and CEO of Phillips Petroleum, gave his employees the right kind of coaching on how to respond to merger-related changes:

> We paralyze ourselves if we put our plans and good ideas on hold "until things get back to normal." We can't afford to fall into the trap of thinking about the present as a temporary period of discomfort that will go away if we just wait patiently ... Our challenge is not to sit around and wait until the storm blows over, but to learn how to work in the rain.[1]

3. *Arrange for participation and involvement.* Participation is critical to a successful change effort, but indiscriminate participation creates its own set of problems.

---

[1] Pete Silas, "Our Performance Today Will Determine Our Future," PHILNEWS, July 1986.

Conventional wisdom has held that participation brings ownership of ideas and that ownership generates commitment. This argues that instead of trying to force change down people's throats, there is a need to get them involved in the process of designing the change and planning how it is to be implemented.

This is not to say, though, that people should be sourced for their ideas and opinions automatically. If they don't know about the subject at hand, there is reason to question how constructive their ideas might be. When they don't really have much at stake in the outcome, their contribution may be questionable. Further, if the person soliciting their involvement doesn't really give a hoot about what they have to say, it might be better not to even go through the motions.

Participation is valuable when the people involved are capable of contributing worthwhile ideas. It can be a productive exercise when the participants are able to help define and solve key problems.

But mere participation for participation's sake can be highly dysfunctional. It can waste people's time and energy and result in an overall weaker game plan for change.

So the key to effective participation is involving the right people. When that happens, people do end up with a better understanding of how complicated the situation is. And if there are no perfect solutions (which there almost never are), then they are probably going to be much more inclined to live with "reasonable" solutions that are fair minded and that they have helped to shape and bring to life.

4. *Provide a clear sense of direction.* In the disordered environment of mergers and acquisitions, where changes themselves are constantly being changed, employees need an aiming point. They need a target to shoot at.

Otherwise, there is a tendency to wallow or flounder in the waves of change. People will resist the changes because they cannot determine where the new forces are carrying them.

It's one thing for a military commander to march his troops across an icy, rugged mountain range with their knowledge that on the other side will come victory over the enemy and glory for the individual soldier. It's something else altogether to give only the order, "Okay, men, today you climb mountains and crawl through snow and ice. Move out!"

There are two very important components to the needed sense of direction.

First, there need to be very short-range objectives that are specific, highly structured, and vigorously promoted. But at the same time there needs to be an overarching goal, something that people can orient toward well into the future. There is much less resistance to change when people can view the changes as part of their pursuit of a vision.

This visionary objective gives employees something they can get excited about. It needs to be articulated by the leader, and should be the sort of challenging goal that might be defined as a unique mission, calling, or purpose that really inspires people.

This is the kind of thing that can justify for employees all of the upheaval, confusion, stress, and destabilization that change brings. In other words, vision is what allows people to conclude that all the effort and headaches associated with change are worth the price.

5. *Give leadership.* When things are changing, when an organization is destabilized, people need someone to follow. It has to be someone they have confidence in, someone they feel has the ability to lead them out of the struggle safely. When leadership is missing, resistance festers and spreads.

All too often when a company is being acquired and merged some of the key people—who are the best leaders—leave the scene. Others get reassigned, with the result being a lot of people who feel they have been left leaderless. They easily fall into the ranks of the passive resisters.

6. *Move rapidly in making the changes.* A key step in managing past resistance to change is to expedite the change process.

This is not to advocate recklessness or a haphazard approach. But very often the people in charge decide they don't want to overwhelm their employees with change. So out of the spirit of compassion or misguided sensitivity, they put together what sounds like a very logical argument for staging changes in a fairly slow-paced or measured fashion.

On the surface this sounds like a very humanitarian approach. The problem is, it simply doesn't work.

Almost always, people instinctively know when this is happening, and they end up feeling like they're kind of hanging in the wind. They intuitively realize that the changes aren't all made and that things aren't "finished." This adds tremendously to the uncertainty of the situation.

So while the people in charge may elect to move slowly and thus not overwhelm their people with change, they are likely to overwhelm them with ambiguity.

The most promising approach is to make the needed changes rapidly and get them over with. Sure, it should be done in an informed fashion and not willy-nilly. But the company should move with real dispatch rather than dragging things out.

So often what people really resist is the sluggish pace of change, or the ambiguity and uncertainty that accompany the change because everything is proceeding so slowly.

The kindest sword is the one that cuts quickest and cleanest. So don't "hack around," making the changes over a long period of time. That just prolongs the agony. It creates more pain and suffering, while also slowing down the healing process.

It's not hard to understand why people would resist that.

7. *Provide appropriate training.* When people have doubts about their own ability to perform up to par in a new situation or under a new set of expectations, their primary defense may be to resist the changes that are threatening. As mentioned earlier, it's human nature not to want to set ourselves up for failure.

Frequently, people are against change not because they are opposed to it per se, but rather because they lack the skill, talent, or simply the understanding needed to cope with it very well. If they are given the necessary training and coaching on how to handle change effectively, the resistance can disappear.

All too often, though, companies are acquired and merged without employees ever being given sufficient guidance or assistance on how to do things the new way.

To begin with, people are likely to need help in understanding merger dynamics together with training on how to manage transition and change. It's a very different process from "maintenance management" or taking care of the status quo.

Ordinarily, there also are technical matters that are handled differently from one company to the next, and if they are to be synchronized, employees can benefit from training.

Invariably, the parent company and its acquisition will need to reconcile numerous formal policies and procedures as well as a variety of unwritten practices. Rather than have people struggle along for months trying to figure out on their own how to do things according to the new game plan, special training sessions should be scheduled very early in the merger integration process.

The area where a specialized kind of training is almost always needed, and is usually ignored completely, has to do with the complex area of corporate culture. In spite of the fact that corporate culture has a pervasive and profound influence on employee behavior and the way business is conducted, acquiring companies take it largely for granted. They more or less assume that those personnel who are being acquired and integrated will manage to "catch on" and get the hang of it without any help from the parent firm.

The truth of the matter is that companies find it difficult even for themselves to identify all the important, deeply held beliefs and corporate values that comprise its culture.

How much harder, then, is it bound to be for newcomers to really understand what's going on and why? Granted, having more of an outsider's perspective, people from the acquisition will quite readily perceive certain values and beliefs that people in the parent company are oblivious to. But they need to be provided carefully orchestrated training—indoctrination, if you will—on the new corporate culture within which they will be expected to operate. In the absence of such training, acquired company personnel are likely to be accused of resisting change when, in fact, they are just doing what comes naturally, unaware that it is not in sync with what the parent company expects.

8. *Create a supportive environment.* Change is accepted by people more readily in a nurturing, supportive environment. When this kind of atmosphere exists, people are more willing to take some risks and experiment with new ways of doing things.

If they feel threatened, insecure, or vulnerable, they become inhibited. They don't want to go out on a limb. They become more cautious, more tentative and, quite frankly, more likely to fail.

So the people in charge need to concentrate on *shaping* people's behavior instead of *grading* people's behavior.

This is almost an attitudinal issue. People very quickly get a feel for the boss' or leader's stance. They can intuitively grasp whether or not there is much safety in trying to do things the new way, and maybe failing or at least falling short to some degree.

The atmosphere needs to be encouraging and affirming. In the words of *The One Minute Manager*, there is a need to "catch people doing something right."[2]

That creates an environment where people flourish, and where change can take root. The boss needs to give positive strokes merely for movement in the right direction instead of waiting for people to get it perfect.

9. *Monitor the change process carefully.* Another key point in overcoming resistance to change is to keep tabs on the situation.

More than likely there will be problems that develop. Certainly if the change is very complex or very involved, there will be some glitches. If these problems aren't sniffed out and met head-on— that is, sensibly addressed by top management—then the people are going to bow up. They are going to become more resentful. Furthermore, they will view the problems as tangible evidence that the changes were poorly conceived, destructive, and less effective than the old way of doing things.

So managers and executives should really keep a finger on the pulse of things in terms of how well the changes are going, or how well the new approach is working.

Essentially, what is being said here is that top management should go looking for trouble and be particularly alert to bad news. People should be encouraged to come forth with their complaints, concerns, and gripes—that's how management ends up with the information needed to fine-tune the situation.

Sometimes the information that comes forth when people gripe and complain or offer suggestions may be very faulty. It may be off target, and a very parochial viewpoint.

Nevertheless, if that is the perspective or the viewpoint of the people who have to live with the changes and who will carry a

---

[2]Kenneth Blanchard and Spencer Johnson, *The One Minute Manager* (New York: William Morrow, 1982), p. 40.

large part of the responsibility for making the changes work, then those opinions are important.

Success at overcoming resistance to change is heavily dependent on keeping the information channels open. The company should do whatever is possible to keep the communication flowing regarding what's working, what's not, and what's needed.

If people don't feel comfortable coming forth to express their problems or report the difficulties they're having, resistance is just driven underground. The result is a bunch of employees who may mouth the party line before top management, but who behind their backs proceed to undercut the changes and keep them from working.

10. *Exhibit managerial courage.* Sometimes managers will find that in their particular part of an organization the change isn't working well at all. There will be feedback from their people, or they may observe firsthand, that there are some very significant problems. It is entirely possible that some of the change will have been ill-conceived or poorly implemented.

Maybe those changes were force-fed to the managers. Maybe they didn't have any say-so in deciding whether or not the changes should be made in the first place. Perhaps these were directives that came down from on high, with the managers simply being charged with the responsibility for implementing them and making them work.

When they aren't working, or when some real fine-tuning is needed, managers have to have the nerve or managerial courage to report problems to their superiors. And they may not want to hear that upstairs.

It takes real inner strength to blow the whistle on a problem and to ask for what's needed. It may be, though, that this is the key step in handling the resistance.

As mentioned earlier, there are certain instances where change should be resisted. Regrettably, in the merger environment managerial courage is sometimes in short supply. This is understandable, given the fact that the trust level is low and people are concerned about protecting their own careers. But it also helps explain why change is usually undermanaged in merging organizations.

COACHING POINTS

1. Expect resistance.

2. Invite resistance. The secret is to get it out into the open. Then, at least, you are in a position to analyze it and work toward overcoming it.

3. Reward/reinforce the right attitudes and behavior. "Shape" people toward embracing the changes.

4. Respect the fact that resistance is diagnostic—that is, when resistance becomes extreme, something is not being done right. The phenomenon of resistance to change is sort of like body temperature in that it can go too high, or too low. When resistance is too high, there will be casualties—for example, people quit, productivity is crippled, there may be a union drive, and so forth. If resistance is virtually nonexistent, it probably connotes an organization that is overstabilized and too complacent.

CHAPTER SIX

Managing the Team-Building Process

Teamwork is one of the factors that heavily influence the level of organizational effectiveness. And one of the reasons companies lose momentum and productivity in the merger/acquisition environment is because team play is disrupted.

The customary changes that occur in firms that are being acquired and merged can interfere with a work group's performance in a variety of ways. This is highlighted if a comparison is made between changes that might impact on an athletic team and those that mergers bring to bear on a corporate work team.

The parallels are shown below:

Sports Team	Business Team
New coach	New boss
New players on the team	New employees merged or added
Old players dropped from the team	Employee bailouts, terminations, and transfers; loss of group resources
Players (possibly both old and new) playing different (unfamiliar) positions	Employees, at various levels, who are confused, uncertain, or unskilled in their new roles
New playing field	Relocation or reassignment
New style of play	Different culture, norms, procedures, etc.

(continued)

Sports Team	Business Team
New standards for making the team	Changes in the performance appraisal program; new reward system; superiors who value a different set of behaviors
New play book	Different goals/objectives, priorities, and plans

If a team (sports or business) is not very effective to begin with, changes such as those listed above have more potential for actually having a positive effect on teamwork.

Maybe an acquisition, for example, needs new blood or a better leader.

Companies and employees can get complacent, too. The organizational shake-up that mergers and acquisitions bring may jolt people out of a rut and produce more effective individual performance as well as enhanced team play.

More commonly, though, merger-related changes damage teamwork. The events listed above cause work groups to regress to a more primitive stage of team development. In the process, overall output diminishes, quality of the work that is produced can suffer, and job satisfaction drops.

It's quite possible for the most effective, highly developed pre-merger teams to show the most slippage in performance when all the changes hit.

Again, think of the parallel in a high-precision, professional athletic team. For example, picture a scenario that has the Dallas Cowboys football team merging with the Oakland Raiders. One head coach goes, the other stays. There are redundancies at virtually every position because there are two full squads. As a result, a sizable number of players are released, and some who are exceptional athletes are retained but switched to different positions. Many people are required to move to another city and start practicing and playing in another geographical setting.

Even more complicated are the issues of reconciling Oakland's looser, more aggressive, and reckless style of play with the Dallas team's culture of finesse and its complicated systems. Dallas is white hat, Oakland players are "outlaws."

It's inconceivable to think that teamwork will not suffer during the merging and integration of the two organizations. There will be power struggles, poor communication, misunderstandings, and much confusion. What an opportunity for the competition!

Management has to work hard to protect and preserve team play during the merger process. Even with that there is almost always a significant amount of damage that occurs, such that rebuilding teams throughout the organization is necessary.

The more the acquisition is resisted by incumbents, and the more there is to be an integration and consolidation of work forces, the more important team building becomes.

Formal team-building projects are aimed at two primary objectives:

1.   Overcoming dysfunctional group and individual behaviors that are a drag on organizational effectiveness.
2.   Realizing more of a team's inherent potential.

Team-building efforts, when designed and conducted by capable professionals, can make outstanding contributions toward:

- Helping people work together compatibly.
- Improving communications.
- Establishing priorities.
- Framing out agreed-upon goals and objectives.
- Working through interpersonal conflict.
- Clarifying roles and responsibilities.
- Building trust and mutual support.
- Addressing various problem areas in team functioning.
- Overcoming resistance to change.
- Identifying a team's individual and collective strengths, plus how those can best be utilized.

STAGES OF TEAM DEVELOPMENT

Teams develop along very predictable lines. There is a growth process that can be shown as a series of stages a group of people progress through in developing into a mature, close-knit, high-performance team (See Figure 4).

As the stages unfold, there are tremendous changes in how the people relate to each other. The problems that are experienced

FIGURE 4: Stages of Team Development

Stage 1
Reconnaissance

Interpersonal relationships are shallow and guarded.

Team members depend on the leader for direction, support, job structure, and definition of the task to be accomplished.

Communications damaged by mask-wearing, skirting issues, hinting, uneven participation, and lack of candor.

Productivity is weak; quality of output suffers because group is ineffective at using its available resources; decisions not adequately challenged, and often are not fully supported; questionable commitment to output and decisions.

Stage 2
Skirmishing and Maneuvering

Power struggles, interpersonal conflict, confrontations, arguments, people taking things personally.

Leader may be challenged, or circumvented; team members vie for influence, power, and visibility.

Tension mounts; energy wasted on internal battles.

Hidden agendas, defensiveness, poor listening, and game-playing interfere with communication.

Productivity deteriorates; team feels bogged down and stalled out; participants reconsider their desire to be a part of the team.

Stage 3
Closing Ranks

Comfortable working relationships; people understand and accept one another.

Power balance (or "pecking order") pretty well resolved.

Energy is channeled along more productive lines.

Openness in expressing feelings, ideas, opinions; team members give one another feedback.

More output, and better quality results.

Stage 4
Elite Corps

Relationships are close and supportive; high level of trust and confidence in teammates.

Leadership and power are handled in a flexible manner to suit the situation at hand; team plays to the individual interests and skills of its members.

Energy level is high; the team inspires itself; no energy wasted on self-protective behaviors or in-fighting; good energy conservation.

Communication is open and honest; disagreement and conflict are encouraged as constructive.

Results reflect synergism and resourcefulness of the group; strong pride in the team's accomplishments.

vary greatly from one stage to the next, too, and this heavily influences what the team is able to accomplish as a work unit.

Managers and executives need to know the stages that are involved in the team development process. First, the stages provide a mental framework for assessing where a team is in terms of its growth and maturity. This makes it easier to anticipate the sort of problems that must be addressed, and has clear-cut implications for the steps that must be taken if the team is to continue its development.

Stage 1: Reconnaissance. At the beginning there is not so much a team as a loose collection of individuals.

People are cautious, guarded, and watchful. Their senses are alert to the subtle messages (both verbal and nonverbal) that might help answer the question, "Where do I belong in this group?" They reconnoiter the social landscape in an effort to get the lay of the land and find their place in the group relative to the others.

This period has been compared to the "ritual sniffing" that occurs whenever animals encounter one another. It is a time of testing, of getting acquainted and sizing up the other parties.

Each person demonstrates his or her usual, very individualistic approach to getting involved with others. Some are eager, impulsive, good-humored, conversational. Others are reserved, taciturn, and perhaps fearful. Some may seek attention, while others move to the fringes of the group.

In Stage 1, mask-wearing and hidden agendas are commonplace. Personal feelings and genuine emotional reactions are typically concealed. Even strong personal opinions are commonly toned down. Generally people stick pretty close to the conventional, established approach. There is a reluctance to suggest major changes or to do anything controversial because of people's uncertainty regarding how the group will handle those sorts of things.

Behavior in this phase of team development is typically cordial and polite, although rather impersonal. Social relationships, on the whole, are shallow—pleasant, maybe, but unrewarding. Social ambiguity is high.

If there is a designated person in charge, he or she will clearly be the central figure. Others watch closely to analyze this person's style, how it's received, and how much tolerance there is for others to disagree, challenge, or otherwise exert influence. This is a primitive team, a dependent group, where members look to the person in charge for direction and definition of the tasks to be addressed.

With the passing of time together, there is an increase in social contact and interpersonal exchange. Nevertheless, people use primarily indirect means to explore others' opinions, values, style, attitudes, and willingness for involvement. This process continues until individuals reach their conclusions regarding what their respective involvement in the team will be.

It may appear to the casual observer that the team is functioning effectively, with a friendly camaraderie between members, and with the group as a whole making impressive progress toward achieving its tasks.

But usually this is only a veneer. It is a misleading surface appearance that comes from the socially appropriate behaviors people have learned to use over the years.

The fact is, in Stage 1 people are more self-oriented than team-oriented. There is more talking than there is good listening. People are more interested in self-protection than self-expression. Team members intellectualize, skirt sensitive issues, and give watered-down opinions. Meetings frequently amount to little more than a series of statements, where one person after another offers an individual viewpoint, showing little care for other people or their views.

At this stage of the game personal weaknesses of team members are studiously ignored or covered up. This is because the group lacks the ability to support the individual or overcome the shortcomings. Mistakes, when they do occur, are frequently used in a negative fashion. That is, they are used as leverage against people rather than as a vehicle for learning. Sensing this, team members seek to conceal their weaker points or vulnerabilities.

Here in the Reconnaissance stage participants frequently have a very limited grasp of what really needs to be done. Goals and objectives are often vague, poorly constructed, and inadequately communicated.

Resources are not used very well at all:

1. Time is wasted on insignificant topics and sidestepping issues.

2. Energy is wasted on mask-wearing and other self- protective behaviors, such as stifling emotions and picking words carefully.
3. There is not enough attention to group process (i.e., how people are working together as a group).
4. The team is not really very well in touch with the competencies of the individual members.

While a relaxed, comfortable atmosphere is common, it can easily evaporate when fundamental issues begin to surface. Problems relative to interpersonal difficulties, lack of commitment, and inadequate procedures can develop very easily, and will when and if the team moves into Stage 2.

Stage 2: Skirmishing and Maneuvering. As the team progresses into this stage, the thinly veiled issues and problems that were previously glossed over now have to be dealt with.

Naturally, team members will have quite different opinions regarding when the time is right for this, just as they will have some incompatible goals and different ideas regarding how to go about resolving the situation.

The politeness and more formal, "nice" behavior exhibited in Stage 1 gives way to obvious disagreement and conflict in Stage 2. Feelings and emotions that were well controlled, if not completely hidden, now are ventilated. Frequently they are even intensified due to the more competitive atmosphere that prevails in Skirmishing and Maneuvering.

This is a stage of difficulties that are primarily power oriented and interpersonal in nature. It is here that team members often feel the group is floundering.

Paradoxically, Stage 2 activities usually are hard evidence that the team is working through some fundamental issues and growing up.

Still, this phase is quite disconcerting to some people. Those individuals who dislike conflict and confrontation, in particular, are likely to worry about the team splintering or otherwise deteriorating. But the problems of Stage 2 are valuable evidence that the team is on the proper pathway toward growth. Here again we have an example of a situation where things have to "get worse before they get better."

The more aggressive and assertive team members will skirmish actively. Some may actually enjoy fencing with each other. But people of a different bent may rely on cunning and maneuvering to position themselves.

Still others will feel compelled to try to control the conflicts. If these harmonizers or peacemakers are unsuccessful, they may opt out or "punt," moving to the sidelines and condemning the actions of others.

Sometimes, if they are astute and manipulative enough, they may manage to maneuver the entire group away from the conflict and, regrettably, back into Stage 1 (for example, by shaming the aggressors, exhorting everyone to be "reasonable," etc.).

The secret to making it through Stage 2 successfully is working through conflicts and differences rather than glossing over or ignoring them. When teams seek to sidestep the tough questions of Stage 2 instead of confronting them head-on and working through them, the team's future is in jeopardy. It may appear that the team is moving ahead, while unresolved issues remain to gnaw away at the team's effectiveness.

Stage 2 reveals participants trying to work out the pecking order in more specific terms. As people try to stake out their turf, power plays develop. Individuals jockey for position and seek to determine just exactly what their range of influence will be. Team members get more personally invested in relationships with certain people, forming alliances and cliques. The confusion and distrust of Stage 2 remain good breeding grounds for hidden agendas and selfish motives.

At the root of almost all Stage 2 issues are the "role and control" questions:

1. Who will be in charge?
2. How will control be exercised?
3. What will happen to "delinquents"?
4. What are the limits of my authority?
5. How much "informal power" can I wield?
6. Where are the boundaries of my job?

These are the questions that must be resolved for team members to proceed into the more advanced stages of development.

The team leader or "boss," whose authority was quite readily accepted in Stage 1, now must qualify himself or, so to speak, earn his spurs. His behavior, his style and degree of effectiveness, will be carefully scrutinized and evaluated by the other team members.

The rest of the team will "take his measure," and if he comes up short, the power that is vested in his position will begin to erode. People will begin to undercut his authority, work around him, and otherwise subvert the formally established chain of command.

Team members want to pin down just exactly what the role of the team leader is going to be. (That is usually fundamental in assessing their own range of influence, authority, freedom, etc.)

Because so much of the energy and attention in a Stage 2 group is devoted to infighting, the team frequently is not particularly effective in getting its basic job done. Countless hours are wasted in unproductive meetings where people spar with one another, play games, offer false support, agree to things they don't really accept, interfere with each other's efforts, and generally prove themselves unable to make decisions or get closure. Issues that supposedly were resolved get reopened by people who want to renegotiate. Nerves are on edge. Tempers previously well controlled now flare. People are prone to overstatements and heavily biased viewpoints.

A common characteristic of Stage 2 is that people fight (and try to change) those things they don't like in the situation and in other people. They may feel outmaneuvered and manipulated, with the result being that they scramble to reposition themselves. Egos get in the way of work, and feelings often get hurt.

It is during Skirmishing and Maneuvering that people frequently begin to question their desire to be a part of the team. They may look for escape routes. The commitment to the team that perhaps was easy to assert in Stage 1 now appears to come at a cost, and people reconsider the situation. Negative stereotyping gets in the way of dealing with things objectively, and polarization occurs.

Parent companies are often surprised in Stage 2 when people who supposedly were "on the team" get upset and quit, or threaten to do so. Stage 2 problems like this provide good evidence that the polite, superficial way of handling things in Stage 1 leaves many important issues unresolved.

Progress through this stage comes when people achieve a deeper understanding and respect for each other, and succeed in building a team climate that permits people to express their differences and reach common understandings.

The foundation for this is trust. The manager who wants to overcome the difficulties of Stage 2 will likely find it very helpful to spend time, one on one, with subordinate team members. Efforts to develop more of a personal relationship can be quite beneficial. For example, a manager may ask an employee and spouse to dinner. Even just having extended conversations during the course of the work day can help reach a better mutual understanding. Such dialogue can enable people on the team to resolve philosophical differences and explore the specifics of their working relationships.

Ordinarily, Stage 2 is a difficult time for large group team-building efforts. Working with individuals or small subgroups, such as duos or trios, usually is the most productive approach until the total team has progressed to Stage 3.

The value of Stage 2 struggles becomes apparent when the team itself, its integrity as a unit, takes precedence over the self-interest or individual gratification of its members. In the postmerger integration period, that can be slow in coming. Far too often power struggles continue many months after the merger papers have been signed. Sometimes Skirmishing and Maneuvering will go on for several years.

Stage 3: Closing Ranks. Those teams that successfully emerge from Stage 2 are typically energized and eager to approach their work in a more organized fashion.

Now that interpersonal relationships have been squared away, objectives have been agreed upon, and the issues of power and control have been satisfactorily resolved for the time being, the team enjoys a new level of confidence and is much more willing to experiment.

Riskier issues can be tackled now, as this is a time of regrouping and closing ranks. Team members have learned in Stage 2 that they can confront sensitive issues, allow conflict and confrontation, and survive to become an even more cohesive team.

Now it is considered legitimate, even important, to give feedback to one another. There is more candor, more honest sharing of feelings, and more trust.

Personal issues can be addressed—first, because the Stage 3

group simply steps up to problems in a more open, willing fashion. Also, there is a new respect for how people's feelings impact on the team's effectiveness.

Now the team becomes much more attentive to the process by which it functions. Participants have a renewed (and strong) level of commitment to making the team work, and one of the ways this is manifested is through an introspective posture. The team carefully examines its operating methods, problem-solving approach, and procedures. For the first time, it has become a self-critiquing unit.

Now the team purposefully strives to develop the skills and establish the procedures that will enable it to operate with more precision and achieve greater effectiveness. Listening improves. There is more respect shown for teammates' contributions. Also the group will begin to develop its own vernacular or "verbal shorthand." The team's slang phrases reflect a new level of camaraderie and "in group" behavior.

Probably for the first time, the team begins to impress itself with what it can achieve. This success whets its collective appetite for still more effective team play. The group is beginning to nurture itself.

Traditional team-building efforts have a far higher probability of success in Stage 3 than in Stage 2. The actual need is greater during Skirmishing and Maneuvering, but people are generally too troubled as individuals to get with the program. There is too much fear and mistrust in Stage 2 for total group team building to be really productive.

In Stage 3, by contrast, there is a natural coalescing that can aid (and be aided by) traditional team building. People want to close ranks. The team is truly interested in itself as a group.

The contribution of individual team members is straightforwardly discussed and evaluated in this phase. There is a strong search for greater economy of effort, for a more streamlined approach. The team invests much more time now than ever before in critiquing individual and overall team performance, creative planning, identifying options and alternatives, and so on. It is this Stage 3 attention the team gives to its working methods that enables it to move beyond the marginally effective or merely satisfactory ways of operating to become a truly outstanding team.

As people close ranks and the team becomes more competent, cohesive, and resourceful, its results improve. This enhances the group's pride and esprit de corps. It also results in more recognition from external parties.

Team members thus become more emotionally committed to the team and more protective of it.

Stage 4: Elite Corps. It is a relatively rare and highly rewarding experience to be part of a Stage 4 group.

There is a sense of belonging and camaraderie that enriches the lives of team members and that all participants seek to protect. Relationships are close and supportive. This nurturing social climate allows individuals to flourish and engage their talents to a maximum degree.

The team can now truly function as an elite corps because of this rare social climate that empowers the individual members. The team is now a synergistic unit—the whole is greater than the sum of its parts. This is team play in its truest sense.

Stage 4 teams are highly self-aware. That is, the group understands and respects the needs as well as the capabilities of each person, and uses that information in a constructive fashion. The team is open, authentic, and genuinely concerned with the well-being of each team member.

Individual energies and talents are invested in the team's effort rather than in self-serving pursuits. This is possible because participants are fully confident that the team will, in turn, protect their individual interests.

The trust level is very high and communication is very effective. Team members feel free to disagree. In fact, constructive conflict is seen as necessary and helpful.

In elite corps teams, the leadership issue is characterized by a remarkable degree of flexibility. It is the situation, rather than protocol, that determines who will step forth to give the team the precise leadership needed at the moment.

Again, this is possible because the group has very good insights into its strengths, and can adapt to circumstances in such a way as to play to those strengths most effectively.

This does not mean, however, that there is excessive role ambiguity or confusion regarding who's in charge. To the contrary, the team members understand their respective roles, and each person's contribution is seen as distinctive. The team leader acknowledges the need to involve the other members in significant matters. The interaction is collaborative rather than competitive or authoritarian.

Relations between team members are informal, although there is a strong personal regard for each other. The spirit of the team supersedes such matters as differences in rank.

The close relationships of the participants commonly extend beyond the boundaries of the team and its particular business activity, reaching into the personal lives of the team members.

Teams that manage to develop to this stage of maturity are both admired and emulated by other groups. Elite corps personnel carry themselves with pride, too, but remain self-critiquing and alert to the processes by which they operate.

The Stage 4 team continues to seek improvement, refinement, and further utilization of its resources.

It is important for the elite corps team to develop open relationships with other groups external to the team. Team members also need to be aware that the intimacy or closeness of the team could conceivably result in arrogance and insular attitudes.

Some groups never progress past Stage 1, Reconnaissance. Teams with high turnover, or groups of people who meet rarely and have little time to interact with each other, will find it difficult to develop into the more advanced stages.

Of course, that may not be a particular problem, if the group's task does not really require much teamwork to succeed. Still, Stage 1 groups are not very impressive in terms of work accomplishment.

The last point also holds true for teams that get stuck in Skirmishing and Maneuvering (Stage 2). Here, too much energy is frittered away on infighting. The disunity, the lack of coordinated effort toward achievable goals, gets in the way of good results.

Stage 3 groups are stabilized enough to deliver quite respectable levels of work accomplishment. It is the elite corps team, though, that consistently produces impressive results.

The problem is, groups have to touch all the bases on their way to Stage 4. It seems there are no shortcuts, for example, from Stage 1 or Stage 2 to the elite corps team and its peak productivity.

THE TEAM-BUILDING PROCESS

Groups advance and become more highly developed teams only if their members are willing to have them move forward. And progress always has a price. Movement through each stage requires that the team members give up something in order to progress to the next higher level of performance.

An initial step in the team-building process is for managers to achieve a good understanding of the predictable stages of team development. Secondly, managers need a firm grasp on just what it is that interferes with team development, or what makes up the obstacle course through which groups will need to navigate enroute to becoming a high-performance team.

It is not easy to take a group of people and develop them into an elite corps team. This is particularly true when one is having to struggle with all the complicated dynamics of being acquired and merged.

There are several essential elements in the team-building formula. The most fundamental requirements are the following:

- Trust.
- Mutual support.
- Openness; a willingness to make oneself vulnerable.
- A willingness to confront others, and be confronted; legitimacy of conflict.
- Goals/objectives that are clearly defined and mutually agreed upon.
- Effective leadership.
- Functional procedures.
- Self-critique; attention to group process.

Blockages to team development occur at every stage. Some are the fault of team members. Others have to be blamed on the team leader.

Since managers ordinarily function as team leaders for their own groups and serve as members of other teams (such as their superiors' crew of direct reports), it is important to identify the things one can do to foster team development both as a team member and a team leader.

At the most basic level, the team member must be committed

personally to team play. The team leader, in turn, must be committed to team building.

Beyond that, the following guidelines are offered for each of the four stages:

Player/Member	*Coach/Leader*
Stage 1: Reconnaissance	
Get involved; participate	Encourage involvement; engineer participation
Play your position	Assign specific positions (i.e., define jobs)
Be willing to ask for help	Listen for requests for help, and reinforce such requests
Accept help, coaching, and leadership	Give help, coaching, and leadership
Find out what's expected of you (e.g., "playing style")	Communicate expectations and standards of performance
Open up; make yourself vulnerable; communicate	Ask for input; solicit feedback; role model openness
Get to know your teammates	Hold team meetings; help people get acquainted
Encourage, reinforce, and nurture teammates	Encourage, reinforce, and nurture the players
Trust your teammates and coach	Trust your players/team members
Be trustworthy	Be trustworthy
Stay with the team	Keep the team intact
Take personal risks	Encourage and reinforce risk-taking
Pay attention to group process	Schedule time to critique group process
Stage 2: Skirmishing and Maneuvering	
Help your teammates look good and succeed	Be fair; don't play favorites or let yourself be "brown-nosed"
Play for the team, not for yourself	Reward team play rather than grandstanding and self-centeredness
Seek clarification of where you fit into the team	Provide the necessary clarification of roles; help sort out the questions of power, authority, and influence
Face up to problems with teammates, and work them through	Resolve conflicts; keep them out in the open

(continued)

PlayerlMember	Coach/Leader
Compete with yourself, not with your teammates	Don't foster troublesome, intrateam competition
Respect the needs of others	Pay attention to the different needs of individuals
Strive for balanced involvement of yourself; don't dominate, and don't run for cover	Keep people involved; prevent bullying as well as opting out
Have the courage to disagree	Legitimize disagreement
Level with teammates, be candid yet nonjudgmental	Level with the players; be candid yet nonjudgmental
Respect the value of differences in players and their points of view; look for unique contributions teammates can make	Encourage players to reveal their differences as people and in their points of view; capitalize on team member difference instead of striving for look-alikes
Take your complaints to the person, or to the group, but not to others "behind the back"	Don't let players manipulate you into a private meeting regarding their problems with a teammate; insist that problems be brought out on the table, or worked out by the two parties privately

Stage 3: Closing Ranks

Abide by the game plan; follow procedures	Communicate the game plan; give structure and direction
Don't get lazy and too contented; help keep the team from going flat	Don't let the team get complacent; push for further growth and development
Find new, appropriate risks to take; experiment	Challenge the group; "rock the boat"

Stage 4: Elite Corps

Assume leadership when you are the one best qualified	Let the person best qualified "call the plays"; share power and authority without feeling threatened
Don't lose touch with other groups or individuals external to the team	Bring in outsiders to stimulate new thinking and broaden perspectives
	Provide vision
	Challenge the team toward excellence

Because team building is a complicated process, with many sensitive issues involved, it should proceed under the guidance of a skilled facilitator who is external to the organization. This is particularly true in the highly charged work climate that mergers produce.

Success usually calls for total support of the effort by the team leader, and a sustained commitment to the team-building process. A one-shot effort at team development may be constructive in certain respects, but it can also result in complications. Better to stage the team-building project over a period of weeks or months, with large chunks of time (two or three days) being devoted to each session.

Team building is not a panacea for the wide variety of merger problems that can develop. But the lack of teamwork, both at the executive level and in the middle management ranks, certainly accounts for a generous number of merger failures that have occurred over the years.

CHAPTER SEVEN

Managing Differences in Corporate Culture

The biggest obstacle to successful merger integration is conflicting corporate cultures. The disturbing statistics of merger/acquisition failures document the problem: Between one-half and three-fourths of the deals that are done never measure up to original expectations.

The companies find they can't live together. Sometimes they stay together, only to fight and feel miserable because their organizational values and lifestyles are incompatible.

CORPORATE CULTURE: THE ORGANIZATION'S PERSONALITY

Just what is "corporate culture"? Why is it so important? How does it exert such a profound influence over an organization and the way employees think, feel, and act?

If you want the cleanest, most straightforward definition of corporate culture, think of it as *corporate personality*.

Usually, when we think of personality, we think of the individual person. That's a good place to start. Think for a minute or two. And identify three things that, in your opinion, represent very fundamental, core aspects of your personality. You might conclude, "I'm a true extrovert," or "I'm a wallflower." Perhaps you see yourself as highly aggressive, or as having a very understated personality. Maybe integrity is a hallmark of your makeup as a human being, or possibly you take pride in your genuine empathy for others.

Just off the top of your head, what comes to mind as two or three traits, characteristics, or attributes that you think are keys to your personality makeup?

Then, ask yourself how easy it would be for you to take one, two, or all of those traits and turn them 90 or 180 degrees. Could you remake yourself in terms of those characteristics? How easy would it be to overhaul your personality so that core dimensions such as these no longer describe or fit you?

There is a basic assumption about people that can be made here: People don't change.

The conventional wisdom is that the individual personality has crystallized to an amazing degree by the time a child is school age. Agreed, a child continues to develop and fine-tune the personality through adolescence and even into adult years. But it's the sameness of the personality, the constancy, that is so striking as the years go by.

People can usually look at their own children, or maybe certain aspects of their own personality, and say, "This child of mine seems to have come into the world made this way or that way," or "I've been that way as long as I can remember."

It is very hard to change people. When someone says, "I don't like this thing about me, I don't like my personality, and I think I'm going to change it," that person has a heavy-duty job to perform. Even if the individual says, "Well, that's probably true. I'll get some special help from a psychologist, or I'll get some coach, psychiatrist, teacher, or whoever, to work with me in changing this central part of my personality makeup," it still will be a very, very sluggish struggle with limited returns.

Personality is extremely resistant to change, and that's why the best predictor of future behavior is past behavior. Granted, it's not a perfect predictor, but it's probably the best single predictor managers will find.

That's why it is unwise to hire people—or marry people, for that matter—with the idea that they can be "rehabilitated" after the fact. This sounds like a rather fatalistic and narrow belief. But there is a second basic assumption about people: People can change.

So when do people change?

It isn't likely to happen to any significant degree when people just decide for themselves that they are going to change. It doesn't occur very much even when they seek assistance from a helper or a professional person.

Personalities change, in significant ways, when the world hits them. When they are impacted by something from the external world, something that absolutely knocks them off the tracks they run on, they can change. Things like the following:

- A brush with death.
- The loss of a child or some other loved one.
- A profound religious experience.
- Coming into sudden wealth (or the reverse).
- A rapid rise to fame.

Events such as these can produce a distinct personality shift, because they make people reframe the way they look at the world, the things they value, what their priorities are, and so on.

THE DIFFICULT TASK OF CULTURE CHANGE

But enough about the individual person—back to the subject of the organization, the corporation, and the corporate personality.

Organizations are like people in many ways. They are made up of people, and lots of times they are talked about with the same terminology. Again, there are two very solid assumptions that can be made:

1.   Companies don't change very much, in and of themselves, in the routine, day-to-day corporate world of going about doing business. Maybe the company grows a little bit, makes a respectable profit, and experiences evolutionary change. But companies are unbelievably consistent and stable in terms of their personality dimensions.

2.   Companies can change. They do change. But usually when this change occurs, it is not because somebody at the top— maybe the executive committee, perhaps the company president—sat down and said, "Look, we don't like this aspect of our personality or corporate culture. And we don't like that aspect either. Let's just reshape it."

Once again, they're taking on a big job. It will be a tremendous struggle.

But if companies can change, and we know they do, when does it happen?

Companies, like people, may show a significant change in corporate personality when the world hits them from the outside. That kind of external impact can come from a merger or from being acquired. Other blows sufficient to reshape corporate culture might be a flood of foreign imports, a devastating legal battle, dramatic technological changes, key governmental actions, and maybe even a sweeping reorganization of a firm.

Major changes in the real world in which the corporation has to live, work, and make a profit can produce meaningful changes in personality.

Once again, though, there has to be something strong enough or meaningful enough to cause an organization to question its priorities or reexamine its values. Plus, there must be a new set of "reinforcers" strong enough to support significant shifts in the way the organization collectively thinks and behaves.

Many companies go through major reorganizations and never experience any culture change whatsoever. And, of course, there are firms that do get hit by powerful forces such that they should change and adapt, but they never do. Sometimes these companies die. Sometimes they end up part of the merger/acquisition casualty statistics, precisely because in the collision of cultures they lose their psychological identity and never recover.

Much is being written about corporate culture these days. One result of this is that some of the popular thinking in corporate circles seems to be, "Well, if we don't like our culture, we'll just go forth and change it."

There are a lot of senior executives who are kidding themselves.

Fortune magazine carried a feature story on the subject, with the authors concluding:

> Corporate culture is real and powerful. It's also hard to change, and you won't find much support for doing so inside or outside your company. If you run up against the culture when trying to redirect strategy, attempt to dodge; if you must meddle with the culture directly, tread carefully and with modest expectations.[1]

---

[1] Bro Uttal, "The Corporate Culture Vultures," *Fortune*, October 17, 1983, p. 72

Deal and Kennedy, in their popular book, *Corporate Cultures*, make much the same sort of observation. Their comment is that changing corporate culture "costs a fortune and takes forever."[2]

Now, it's very important to distinguish between change, in general, and meaningful changes in the corporate personality. A fact of organizational life is that companies are constantly changing certain habits and practices.

Individuals, too, develop new skills, learn new routines, develop new perspectives. But alterations in surface behavior, even new ways of looking at certain things, are not necessarily any good proof whatsoever that personality (or corporate culture) has been changed.

An organization's personality forms over many years, from many shaping influences. And we can't change our personality— either as individuals or as organizations—just because we want to do it or see a need to do it.

The existing personality became what it is due to strong reasons, powerful forces. And there will be many strong reinforcers for keeping it as it is. One of the best indicators of whether or not culture is undergoing change will be the level of "resistance" that is seen and felt. Efforts to change personality generally produce a significant amount of resistance or psychological soreness. If managers set out to make meaningful changes, and do not encounter resistance, they are not changing culture.

A key function of corporate culture is to bring stability to the organization, just as a key function of personality is to bring stability to the individual. As a result, it is safe to say—in fact, it is very important to say—that culture or personality manages us — much more than the reverse.

The question companies must ask themselves, then, is whether there is a real willingness to provoke the resistance and the conflict that culture change will bring.

Will top management see the culture change effort through to completion?

Culture is the critical barrier to change. And the stronger the culture in the first place, the harder it is to change it. Just as the more ingrained a personality trait is, the harder it is to reshape.

---

[2]Terrence Deal and Allan Kennedy, *Corporate Cultures* (Reading, Mass: Addison-Wesley Publishing, 1982), p. 163.

In the merger integration process, culture typically stands squarely in the way of some of the transition and change. Of course, the function of culture is to protect an organization from willy-nilly responses to fads or short-term fluctuations.

But cultural influences just happen to be the sort of things that can really cause problems when a firm is being acquired and merged.

THE TIME WINDOW FOR CHANGE

Now the good news.

Mergers very often are such a destabilizing event, and have such a powerful impact, that they "break the organizational box," so to speak. Frequently there is a window of opportunity that develops during which management can do some very profound things in terms of reshaping the corporate culture.

But if that opportunity is not seized, the window soon slams shut, or gradually slides shut, as the case may be. If time goes by and nothing much changes, people tend to settle back into their same old behaviors and reembrace the same old beliefs and values.

This says two things. First of all, management has an outstanding opportunity to do some things to a corporate system and its beliefs, priorities, and so forth, on the heels of a merger. There is a superb opening (plus a real responsibility) to come forth and lead the organization into the changes that are needed.

To help make the point, think of a situation where a man happens to break a bone in his body. If it's an arm, even if he doesn't take care of it, if he just ignores it, it won't kill him. More than likely the limb will heal itself.

But if the bone is not set properly, what will happen? It's probably going to grow back deformed, crooked, perhaps weaker. The healing process is very unpredictable and, left without a splint or cast, you don't really know what the arm is going to look like after the bone grows back together.

The same type of thing happens when opportunities for culture change aren't managed in a knowledgeable, strategic fashion. Successful culture change efforts are those that proceed in a deliberate, purposeful fashion—where top management knows where it's headed.

If a merger comes along and shakes up corporate culture, and top management doesn't really know what it wants to change the culture to, it may grow back together but be crippled, deformed, and unable to function in an effective manner.

When companies merge, their differences in culture are usually a major contributor to employees' feelings of oppression and confusion. The situation calls for astute management and deep respect for just how complicated it is to manage personality change.

THE IMPACT OF MERGERS ON CORPORATE CULTURE

There are several aspects of corporate culture that should be considered in the context of understanding the impact that mergers have on an organization.

One of the key elements is a company's value system—its basic beliefs. Another fundamental element is the business environment in which the firm conducts business. Then there are also the heroes of the company, plus its day-to-day routines (rituals) and special ceremonies (rites). Finally, there is the cultural network, the informal communication system within the firm.

Deal and Kennedy maintain that the business environment does more to shape corporate culture than does anything else. Essentially, a company's personality becomes what it is because of the shaping influence of many factors: clients and customers, the competition, the technology that is involved, industry regulations and standards, and the products or services produced.

The many realities of the business world in which a firm operates play a major role in carving out the firm's character and culture. Some aspects of the business environment have a very subtle influence. But as relentless winds and waters can erode jagged boulders to a smooth finish with the passing of years, so are some cultures gradually shaped by constant pressures from the marketplace.

Other, more dramatic forces in the environment may impact the culture the way an earthquake reshapes the terrain—suddenly and destructively.

Mergers affect culture in this profound, sudden, and overwhelming manner. For example, companies frequently acquire firms that come from totally different business environments.

Then the parent company, operating from the assumption that its own success can be replicated in the acquisition by having the target firm approach business in the same fashion, destroys the delicate balance between the acquisition's culture and its business environment.

Corporate Values. The values or basic beliefs are the soul of corporate culture. Employees put their faith in these values, accepting them as the basic answer to "what counts" regarding how business is to be conducted.

A firm's values are its shared beliefs regarding how success—as an individual employee, or total organization—is achieved. Thus, organizational values carry a heavy influence over what people actually do in an organization.

When companies are being acquired and merged, though, employees get the feeling that the props have been pulled out from under their values or basic beliefs. Nobody knows whether those basic concepts will endure, or how they might be changed.

This adds a tremendous amount of uncertainty, and causes people to become confused regarding just exactly what the company wants and what it takes to get ahead in the new corporate scheme of things.

Employees need to know what their company stands for. Without a good feel for the firm's values, they become uncertain regarding what standards to uphold. That, in turn, causes management to be unclear regarding decision making.

All too often the merger integration period is a time during which people have difficulty sorting out priorities. There is confusion regarding which tasks are most important, or what information should be given the most weight in making decisions. Frequently, managers feel torn between doing things the way they have been taught they *should* do them versus the parent company's new way of operating.

The Corporate Heroes. The people who emerge as key role models in an organization do most to sell others on the corporate values. The heroes make the basic beliefs come alive by living them out as they actually go about performing their jobs.

The heroes are the strong, pivotal figures who command the respect and attention of others. They are the men and women whose achievements become known to everybody else in the firm. Their behavior—their escapades and accomplishments—become part of the folklore of the company. Their actions inspire others while also getting across the message about what it takes to succeed in the firm.

But heroes often leave when firms are being acquired and merged. These high-profile people may sell out, bail out, get terminated, lose their position of influence and prestige, or otherwise fall from grace.

There are implicit messages in this for those who remain:

1. If the heroes can't survive, who can?
2. If our best and brightest elect to pack up and move on, should we not follow their lead? After all, they are the role models.
3. If we are not to emulate our old heroes, then who will set the standards and symbolize how one becomes a true success in the new corporate framework?

Rites and Rituals. The corporate routines that employees follow as a matter of habit, without ever questioning them, represent a very important aspect of corporate culture. A wide variety of behaviors and practices can be identified as common rites and rituals:

How people address each other.
Award ceremonies.
How employees "play" together.
The way meetings are handled.
How people talk and act in public.
Standards of dress.
The decision-making process.
Communication patterns in the firm.
Where people park, eat, and office.

Virtually always, merging companies do these types of things differently from one another. In fact, what's acceptable or even encouraged in one organization may be punished in the other.

Invariably, there are enough discrepancies in merging companies' rites and rituals to make many employees uneasy about the situation. Some people will become very tentative until they figure out what is acceptable protocol in the parent company. Also, it is very common to see the acquirer misconstruing the behavior of acquired company personnel.

Certainly mergers disrupt the rites and rituals of corporate life. Employees don't know how to handle themselves. They wonder what is expected of them, and frequently become frustrated and angry when their own company's modus operandi conflicts with the new company's routines.

There is a real need for merger integration training that coaches people in the specific behaviors—the rites and rituals that top management of the merged organization considers appropriate.

In the absence of this, people have to infer what the company wants and expects of them. That leaves too much to guesswork, and causes discomfort for employees. Months go by as they try to figure out how they're supposed to do things. They commit faux pas and embarrass themselves, while offending or annoying others in the parent firm who expect adherence to their established corporate culture.

The Cultural Network. In *Corporate Cultures*, Deal and Kennedy write, "We think that 90 percent of what goes on in an organization has nothing to do with formal events. The real business goes on in the cultural network."[3]

The network is the informal communication system in an organization, the information channel that (a) transmits messages to people throughout the company and (b) helps interpret the significance of the messages for all employees.

People who live and work in an organization eventually learn how the network functions. They become rather savvy and adroit in using it to their advantage. Sometimes it seems that about the only way to get things done or to make sense out of the situation is to use the cultural network.

When companies merge, though, the newcomers to the cultural network are at a real disadvantage. They don't know how to work the new system, and the old system from their prior organization may be short-circuited or just not particularly serviceable anymore.

---

[3]Ibid., p. 86

MANAGING CULTURAL CONFLICT

Any time two organizations are being merged, there will be cultural conflicts that need to be reconciled. Cultural integration needs to be managed, *carefully managed*, instead of leaving it for everybody to work out on their own.

All too often, management never really comes to grips with the situation. Several things may account for this:

1. Management doesn't grasp the critical influence of corporate culture on organizational performance.
2. There is a lack of insight into the cultural differences between two merging firms.
3. Management doesn't really know how to proceed, and just chooses to let nature take its course.
4. Management is preoccupied with other—usually more tangible—matters, such as the financial aspects of the merger.

The reality of the situation, however, is that the success of a merger generally is a function of how well the two organizational cultures have been integrated. And the most important job for management is to manage the cultural integration.

Mismanagement of culture has far-reaching ramifications, and sooner or later they affect the bottom line.

COACHING POINTS

1. Know thyself. Get a fix on your company's culture, preferably well ahead of any merging efforts. Organizational blind spots can wreck mergers, resulting in an acquisition strategy that is doomed to failure at the outset.
2. Get to know the other firm's culture—in a hurry! If you do that, you will understand why they are doing (and not doing) certain things now, and you will know what you are likely to see them doing in the future.
3. Determine the most significant conflict points between the two cultures (i.e., where is culture change or "corporate therapy" going to be needed?). It helps to know where trouble is coming from when one is planning a problem-solving strategy.
4. Analyze *other* aspects of culture (in either firm) that should

be changed, given that the merger may create a significant window of opportunity to do so.

5. Think hard about this idea of changing corporate culture in the acquisition. Do you *really* want to take on that struggle? It may make more sense to concentrate on *reconciling* cultural differences—i.e., learn to live together with some basic differences in corporate personalities—instead of attempting to change deep-seated cultural issues in the acquisition.

6. If you are going to try to change corporate culture, then do it right. Get professional help. Involve an external consultant. At least this improves your odds a bit, and a good consultant can help you cope with the frustrations you're going to have.

7. Factor corporate culture into the strategic game plan. Remember, corporate culture manages us.

A company's success at acquiring and merging other firms is measured in numbers, and rightfully so. It's a very digital issue. Dollars and cents. Cash flow, net worth, stock price, market share, P/E ratio, debt figures, tax savings, and so on.

The decision to acquire and merge is based on a financial proposition. And just how well the financial angles have been played is measured, sooner or later, by the bottom line.

There is a problem, though, because so many qualitative issues profoundly affecting financial matters are not readily translated into quantitative terms. As a result, the financial equation has holes in it—gaps where numbers, big numbers, belong. It's time for companies to start calculating them. There is a lot of money slipping through those holes.

Many mergers destined to go sour can be handily salvaged by better management during the integration phase. Many other mergers doomed to financial mediocrity can become outstanding success stories.

The difference rides on the backs of the people who have been put in charge in the two companies—the managers and executives at all levels in the organizational hierarchy. Once the papers are signed, these people make or break the deal. If they are the right people, if they are properly motivated and coached, and if the integration process is carefully monitored, they can make mergers work.

Price Pritchett is Chairman & CEO of Pritchett, LLC. For over 25 years he has been advising CEOs, presidents, and other senior executives on a wide range of strategic matters relating to merger integration and major organizational change. His consulting assignments have taken him to the Far East, Europe, the United Kingdom, and all across the Americas. He has been quoted in *Fortune, Business Week, The Wall Street Journal, USA Today*, most major U. S. city newspapers, and interviewed on CNN, CNBC, as well as numerous corporate cable channels. Dr. Pritchett's 25 books and handbooks have sold a total of 12 million copies, making him one of the best-selling business authors in the U. S.

Books by Price Pritchett

- *After the Merger: The Authoritative Guide for Integration Success (Co-authored with Don Robinson and Russell Clarkson)*

- *Business As UnUsual: The Handbook for Managing and Supervising Organizational Change (Co-authored with Ron Pound)**

- *Carpe Mañana: 10 Critical Leadership Practices for Managing Toward the Future*

- *Culture Shift: The Employee Handbook for Changing Corporate Culture**

- *The Employee Guide to Mergers and Acquisitions*

- *The Employee Handbook for Organizational Change (Co-authored with Ron Pound)**

- *The Employee Handbook of New Work Habits for a Radically Changing World**

- *The Employee Handbook of New Work Habits for The Next Millennium: 10 Ground Rules for Job Success*

- *The Ethics of Excellence*

- *Fast Growth: A Career Acceleration Strategy*

- *Firing Up Commitment During Organizational Change**

- *High-Velocity Culture Change: A Handbook for Managers (Co-authored with Ron Pound)**

- *Making Mergers Work: A Guide to Managing Mergers and Acquisitions*

- *Managing Sideways: A Process-Driven Approach for Building the Corporate Energy Level and Becoming an "Alpha Company"**

- *The Mars Pathfinder Approach to "Faster-Better-Cheaper": Hard Proof From the NASA/JPL Pathfinder Team on How Limitations Can Guide You to Breakthroughs (Co-authored with Brian Muirhead)*

- *Mergers: Growth in the Fast Lane (Co-authored with Robert Gilbreath)*

- *MindShift: The Employee Handbook for Understanding the Changing World of Work*

- *Outsourced: 12 New Rules for Running Your Career in an Interconnected World*

- *The Quantum Leap Strategy*

- *Resistance: Moving Beyond the Barriers to Change*

- *Service Excellence!**

- *Smart Moves: A Crash Course on Merger Integration Management (Co-authored with Ron Pound)**

- *A Survival Guide to the Stress of Organizational Change (Co-authored with Ron Pound)**

- *Team ReConstruction: Building a High Performance Work Group During Change (Co-authored with Ron Pound)**

- *Teamwork: The Team Member Handbook**

- *you²: A High-Velocity Formula for Multiplying Your Personal Effectiveness in Quantum Leaps*

---

* Training program also available. Please call 800-992-5922 for more information about our training, or regarding international rights and foreign translations.

Pritchett Consulting Services

Our consulting group has almost three decades of experience working with organizations from all sectors to successfully plan and implement large-scale strategic change.

We'll help you:

- Design and implement a state-of-the-art merger integration strategy
- Address the people / organizational challenges associated with new information technology
- Radically redesign or make incremental improvements in your organization's key processes
- Develop or reconfigure your processes for effective e-commerce applications
- Address the organization design issues you face due to organizational growth and new business opportunities

> **If you would like to talk to one of our consultants about your unique change-related challenges, please call us at 800-992-5922.**

Introducing Pritchett's Total Merger Solution—eM&A

Pritchett's merger methodology, based on over 25 years of experience, is now available electronically. This easy-to-use format offers organizations the ability to create merger integration competencies in-house.

eM&A gives you the tools to:
- Use the same templates and project formats as Pritchett consultants
- Create your own successful approach using a focused integration plan with proven results
- Form a comprehensive communication plan with monitoring and tracking capabilities
- Identify goals that will help you achieve the highest ROI possible

Call us today to find out how you can own Pritchett's best-of-class methodology to ensure your merger's success.

For more information, call 800-992-5922.

Making Mergers Work

1-19 copies ＿＿＿ copies at $19.95 each

20 or more copies ＿＿＿ copies at $15.95 each

Please reference
special customer number KA1014
when ordering.

Name ＿＿＿＿＿＿＿＿＿＿＿＿＿＿＿＿＿＿＿＿＿＿＿＿＿＿＿＿＿

Job Title ＿＿＿＿＿＿＿＿＿＿＿＿＿＿＿＿＿＿＿＿＿＿＿＿＿＿＿

Organization ＿＿＿＿＿＿＿＿＿＿＿＿＿＿＿＿＿＿＿＿＿＿＿＿＿

Address ＿＿＿＿＿＿＿＿＿＿＿＿＿＿＿＿＿＿＿＿＿＿＿＿＿＿

City, State ＿＿＿＿＿＿＿＿＿＿＿＿＿ Zip Code ＿＿＿＿＿＿＿＿

Phone ＿＿＿＿＿＿＿＿＿＿＿＿＿＿ Fax ＿＿＿＿＿＿＿＿＿＿＿

E-mail ＿＿＿＿＿＿＿＿＿＿＿＿＿＿＿＿＿＿＿＿＿＿＿＿＿＿＿

Purchase order number (if applicable) ＿＿＿＿＿＿＿＿＿＿＿＿＿＿

*Applicable sales tax, shipping and handling charges
will be added. Prices subject to change.
Orders less than $250 require prepayment.
Orders of $250 or more may be invoiced.*

☐ Check Enclosed ☐ Please Invoice

☐ **VISA** ☐ **MasterCard** ☐ **AMERICAN EXPRESS**

Name on Card ＿＿＿＿＿＿＿＿＿＿＿＿＿＿＿＿＿＿＿＿＿＿＿＿

Card Number ＿＿＿＿＿＿＿＿＿＿＿＿＿＿ Expiration Date ＿＿＿＿＿

Signature ＿＿＿＿＿＿＿＿＿＿＿＿＿＿ Date ＿＿＿＿＿＿＿＿＿＿

To order, call: **800-992-5922**
fax: **972-731-1550**
www.pritchettnet.com
or mail this form to the address below

P R I T C H E T T

5800 Granite Parkway, Suite 450 • Plano, Texas 75024